Manual of

Timber Frame Housing

A Simplified Method

Manual of
Timber
Frame
Housing

A Simplified Method

National Building Agency
and Timber Research and Development Association

THE CONSTRUCTION PRESS
LANCASTER   LONDON   NEW YORK

The Construction Press Ltd,
Lancaster, England.

A subsidiary company of Longman Group Ltd,
London. Associated companies, branches and
representatives throughout the world.

Published in the United States of America by
Longman Inc New York.

First published 1980

© Timber Research and Development Association
    and
    The National Building Agency 1980

ISBN 0 86095 8159

Printed in Great Britain at The Pitman Press, Bath.

Contents

Contributors

The following members of NBA and TRADA staff were engaged in the preparation of this Manual:

NBA	TRADA
Tom Darracott	Andy Collett
Robert Maxwell	Michael Keyte
Michael Pickering	John Ollis
Ron Pontin	Steve Prismall
Roger Sadgrove	Trevor Tredwell

together with Paul Marsh, and Shirley Crabtree of the Construction Press. Many others helped both inside and outside these organisations and their contributions are gratefully acknowledged.

Foreword

This Manual has been prepared jointly by the National Building Agency (NBA) and the Timber Research and Development Association (TRADA). The work has been supported by grants from the Department of the Environment.

The Manual is especially aimed at helping those engaged on small projects, in both public and private sectors, where specialist advice is not available. It is designed as an aid for those familiar with ordinary methods of housebuilding, but with no previous experience of timber frame construction.

First principles are explained and advice is given for detailing the construction, for specifying materials, and for building on site. A simple method is set out in the Manual for the design of timber frame dwellings, which ensures structural stability.

If all these recommendations are followed, then complicated calculations are not needed.

The Manual can thus be regarded as a simple but authoritative means of satisfying present-day building standards, and regulations. However, in the Inner London Area there are additional requirements.

It should be noted that the constructional methods and details described do not necessarily represent the only satisfactory way of building timber frame housing. Many proprietary systems have been developed which utilise differing techniques and alternative materials. Such systems are required to provide evidence that they meet the standards of all applicable statutory regulations.

Introduction

This Manual is a simple, basic guide to the use of timber frame in single and two-storey housing. This is a method which is traditional in North America, Scandinavia and other parts of the world.

In the UK its use started to grow about twenty years ago. It is now widely employed by local authorities and developers, especially on large contracts and has thus become accepted as a good method for housebuilding. It is already used for over a tenth of new housing. Yet the principles of timber frame are still not fully known and understood in the building industry.

NBA and TRADA believe that the point has now been reached where timber frame must become part of ordinary housebuilding practice. Correctly used it can provide warm, dry houses, much appreciated by home owners and tenants alike.

It is time, therefore, for the essential principles to be set out as a guide both to those on the drawing board and to those on the site, especially for small contracts.

The NBA/TRADA method set out here is not complicated. It enables those with no experience of timber frame to follow certain simple rules in design and erection, thus ensuring that the best use is made of the timber and other materials.

The rules also ensure that the finished dwellings are built to a good standard. Further, it is shown how current building regulations can be met without difficulty.

It must always be remembered that timber is a natural material. It performs very well provided it is correctly used. (There are many historic timber buildings still in good condition as proof of this.) The method set out in this Manual should not lightly be departed from. A failure might result. The golden rule is, use timber correctly, then the timber will take care of itself. This Manual shows how to put this into practice for timber frame housing.

In some respects the specifications in this Manual are higher than the minimum necessary to meet statutory requirements. For example, three layers of 12.7 mm plasterboard are used to line the separating walls (ie the party walls) between houses, although two layer systems made of one 19 mm and one 12.7 mm layer have been shown by test to meet the fire and sound requirements. The three layer system allows one to use a single thickness of plasterboard throughout the house and should give very reliable results in all circumstances.

Those setting out on their first timber frame project should first read through the whole of the text of this Manual. This will give a general picture of the method and facilitate its practical application.

It must be appreciated that we deal here only with methods special to timber frame construction. We do not go into details of techniques found also in other house-building, such as screeds or roof tiling. We assume that these are familiar to the reader, or that advice and help on these topics may be obtained from other sources.

If, however, problems are found in applying what is set out in this Manual then your TRADA regional officer should be contacted (see inside back cover).

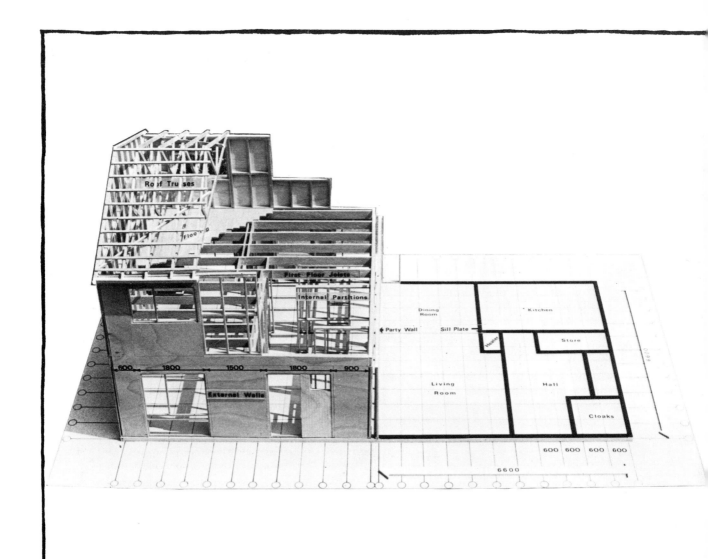

Basic questions people ask

Answers are set out here to nine basic questions such as people with no previous experience of timber frame construction tend to ask. It should be noted that we discuss here only the NBA/TRADA Method. We are not attempting to consider all possible ways of building in timber frame construction.

The questions are as follows:

(1) Why use timber frame construction?

(2) Will it cost more?

(3) What are the basic principles?

(4) Is preservative treatment of the timber needed?

(5) Must factory-made panels be used?

(6) Must dimensional co-ordination be used?

(7) How is the timber frame system erected?

(8) Are there limits to the use of this Manual?

(9) How does it meet Building Regulation requirements?

1. NEED LESS LABOUR ON SITE

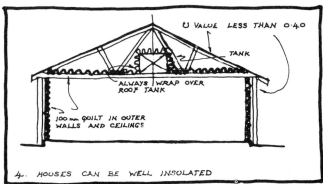

4. HOUSES CAN BE WELL INSULATED

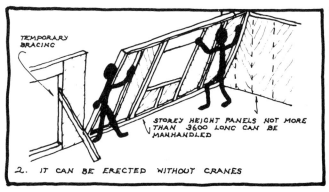

2. IT CAN BE ERECTED WITHOUT CRANES

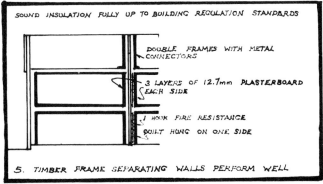

5. TIMBER FRAME SEPARATING WALLS PERFORM WELL

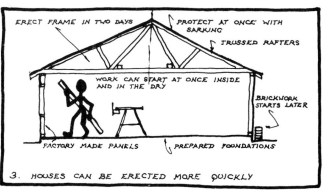

3. HOUSES CAN BE ERECTED MORE QUICKLY

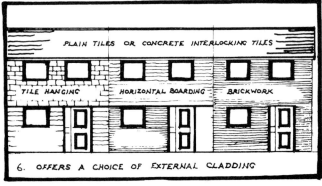

6. OFFERS A CHOICE OF EXTERNAL CLADDING

1 Why use timber frame construction?

There are many reasons for the expanding use of timber frame construction in the UK.

First, it reduces the amount of labour needed on site. This is considerable even when the framing is made up on site. There are further savings where panels are assembled in the factory.

Second, the timber frame can be erected without the use of cranes or other heavy site equipment.

Third, houses can be built more quickly. It is usually possible to put up the whole timber frame for a house within two days. This includes laying sarking felt over the rafters to protect the timber and allow plumbers and electricians to start work at once inside in the dry.

Fourth, houses can easily be finished at low cost to a high standard of thermal insulation. In this Manual the use of 100 mm quilt is recommended, both in the external walls and in the roof space. This can easily save up to a third of the heating costs, when compared with minimum current standards.

Fifth, there are no problems in meeting other current building standards. In particular, timber frame separating walls between dwellings can perform well, both as regards noise reduction and fire. As a result, the method should be fully accepted by local authorities, building societies and insurance companies.

Finally, the method offers a wide choice in the external cladding of houses. This can be in brickwork or concrete blocks, finished like other housing. It can be lightweight, like timber boarding or tile hanging or any of these types of cladding can be combined.

2 Will it cost more?

It is always difficult to compare costs since prices of different building materials fluctuate. But the expanding use of timber frame construction shows it to be competitive in both public and private sectors. This competitiveness is consistent, despite changes in material prices.

With timber frame construction a greater part of the cost goes into materials and components delivered to site than with other types of construction. This is usually more than offset by —

> lower labour content in the superstructure,
>
> less dependence on craft skills,
>
> less delay from bad weather,
>
> easier fixing of plumbing and electrics,
>
> quicker finishing and drying out,
>
> lower overheads per house, because of quicker building,
>
> possible reduced foundation costs due to lighter superstructure.

It is not always easy for builders with no previous experience of timber frame construction to assess what these savings can amount to. However, it should be borne in mind that it will always take time to become sufficiently familiar with a new system to make the most of it.

There are two further points about cost to be remembered when using this Manual.

First, the NBA/TRADA Method is simplified. It avoids the need for special details and structural calculations. As a result, the timber content per house may be higher than in large contracts, designed with specialist advice. But, in compensation, the NBA/TRADA Method allows timber frame construction to be used for small contracts, where such advice is not normally available, and where the overheads for it may not be justified.

Second, the design of the dwelling can have an important effect on cost. The best way to use the NBA/TRADA Method is to *design the dwelling and its timber frame together.* A standard spacing of 600 mm is used for the structure in walls, floors and roofs. This makes most economical use of all the sheet materials, which are in standard widths of 1200 mm (or in some cases 1220 mm, which allows for cutting to exact size with a minimum of wastage). Try to use this spacing to best advantage. Then always check out the dwelling design using the information in Chapter 2.1 of this Manual for lintels, joists and wind loads. *Do this check before the design is finalised.*

It is best not to use dwelling designs based on other building methods. The results are usually wasteful unless they are altered to suit timber frame construction. In some cases this involves only slight changes.

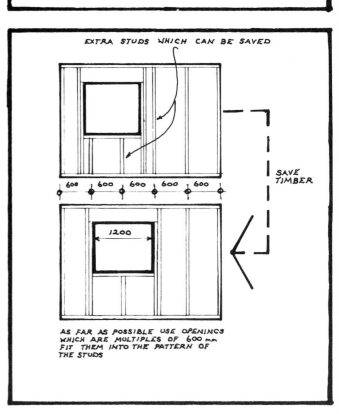

KEEP COSTS DOWN BY DESIGNING THE DWELLING AND ITS TIMBER FRAME TOGETHER

EXTRA STUDS WHICH CAN BE SAVED

SAVE TIMBER

AS FAR AS POSSIBLE USE OPENINGS WHICH ARE MULTIPLES OF 600 mm FIT THEM INTO THE PATTERN OF THE STUDS

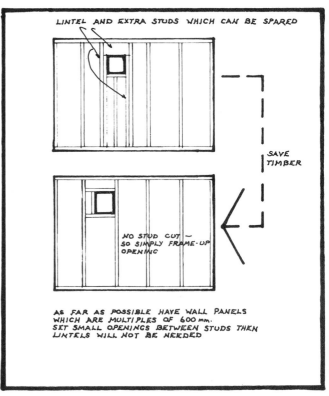

LINTEL AND EXTRA STUDS WHICH CAN BE SPARED

SAVE TIMBER

NO STUD CUT — SO SIMPLY FRAME-UP OPENING

AS FAR AS POSSIBLE HAVE WALL PANELS WHICH ARE MULTIPLES OF 600 mm. SET SMALL OPENINGS BETWEEN STUDS THEN LINTELS WILL NOT BE NEEDED

3 What are the basic principles?

(a) Structure

The NBA/TRADA Method uses floor joists and trussed rafters as in other housing. They are carried on wall frames. These are floor to ceiling level panels, not more than 3.600 metres long so that they can be manhandled. They are made up of verticals, known as studs, set out at 600 mm centres. These are nailed to top and bottom plates. The joists and rafters are kept in line with the studs so the whole structure is kept generally at 600 mm centres.

The same type of frame is used for external walls, for internal partitions carrying floor joists, and for separating walls between dwellings, the latter being made of double frames, one for each house.

External walls are sheathed outside throughout with plywood or other suitable sheeting. This stiffens the structure against wind loads. In some cases, sheathing is used to stiffen certain internal partitions.

Openings are formed with lintels. These are usually made up of double joist material. With large openings, or with heavy loads from upper floors and roofs, hardwood lintels are needed. Lintels are carried on extra studs, known as cripple studs.

All the framing is designed so that simple butt joints and nails are used for assembly. Accuracy in the work is needed, and nailing schedules must be followed – but no special skill in carpentry is required.

(b) Insulation

Ceilings under roofs are insulated as in other housing. Quilt is packed between the studs to insulate external walls. 100 mm quilt is recommended for both.

(c) Keeping external wall frames dry

Two steps are taken to keep external wall frames dry.

First, polyethylene sheet is fixed to the inside face, or aluminium foil-backed plasterboard is used to prevent condensation within the walling. Second, special building paper, known as breather paper, is fixed to the outside face of the plywood sheathing. This prevents any rainwater that may get behind the cladding from wetting the wall panels. But it is not impervious to water vapour, and as a result it will not trap vapour and cause condensation.

Both the vapour barrier on the inside and the breather paper on the outside have important jobs to do. Therefore they must be carefully fixed on site to give complete protection. Any damage must be made good.

(d) Avoiding roof condensation

With the better insulation of ceilings, roof spaces get cold in winter. This increases the risk of condensation on the sarking felt. Because of this, good ventilation of the roof space is needed. Cross ventilation is usual. The total free area should be not less than 1/300th of the ceiling area. Part of this area should be provided in the form of ridge ventilators in cases of sheltered sites and narrow fronted houses. Ensure that roof insulation continues right up to the eaves but does not obstruct the air flow from any eaves ventilators.

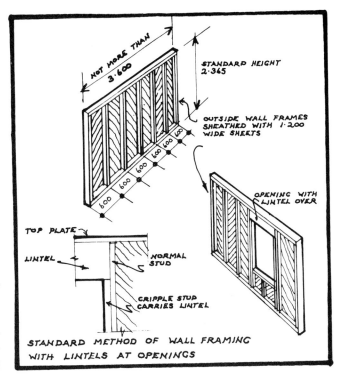

STANDARD METHOD OF WALL FRAMING WITH LINTELS AT OPENINGS

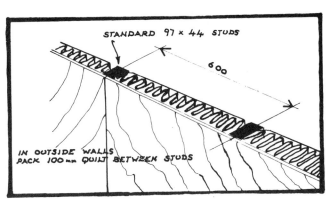

IN OUTSIDE WALLS PACK 100 mm QUILT BETWEEN STUDS

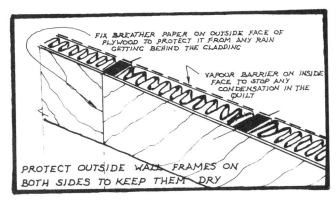

PROTECT OUTSIDE WALL FRAMES ON BOTH SIDES TO KEEP THEM DRY

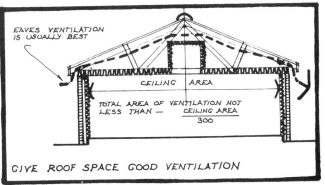

GIVE ROOF SPACE GOOD VENTILATION

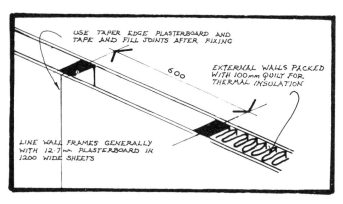

USE TAPER EDGE PLASTERBOARD AND TAPE AND FILL JOINTS AFTER FIXING

600

EXTERNAL WALLS PACKED WITH 100mm QUILT FOR THERMAL INSULATION

LINE WALL FRAMES GENERALLY WITH 12·7mm PLASTERBOARD IN 1200 WIDE SHEETS

(e) Internal linings

A single layer of 12.7 mm plasterboard is used to line the wall panels. This is increased to three layers on frames forming separating walls between dwellings, reducing to two layers for such frames in the roof space (except in Scotland). Ceilings are lined as in other housing.

(f) Floor decking

Tongued and grooved boarding, chipboard or plywood may be used. These materials are applied as in other housing.

(g) Heating, plumbing and electrics

Plumbers and electricians should not be allowed to cut notches or drill holes as they like. The rules are set out in this Manual. As with other housing, no wiring or pipework should go into separating walls between dwellings. The holes made would be liable to let through noise.

(h) Cavity barriers

Because the cavities in timber frame housing contain combustible materials, barriers are required to stop the spread of fire.

Such cavity barriers are needed in separating walls between dwellings, and in external walls.

In external walling, cavity barriers are in timber or mineral quilt depending on types of cladding and their location.

In separating walls, wire reinforced mineral wool blanket is used. This is flexible, so it does not carry noise across the cavity.

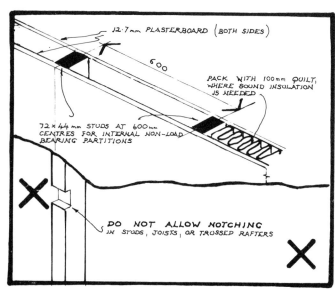

12·7mm PLASTERBOARD (BOTH SIDES)

600

PACK WITH 100mm QUILT, WHERE SOUND INSULATION IS NEEDED

72 × 44mm STUDS AT 600mm CENTRES FOR INTERNAL NON-LOAD BEARING PARTITIONS

DO NOT ALLOW NOTCHING IN STUDS, JOISTS, OR TRUSSED RAFTERS

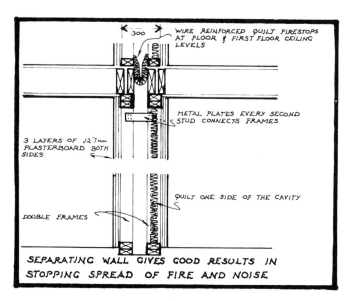

300

WIRE REINFORCED QUILT FIRESTOPS AT FLOOR & FIRST FLOOR CEILING LEVELS

METAL PLATES EVERY SECOND STUD CONNECTS FRAMES

3 LAYERS OF 12·7mm PLASTERBOARD BOTH SIDES

QUILT ONE SIDE OF THE CAVITY

DOUBLE FRAMES

SEPARATING WALL GIVES GOOD RESULTS IN STOPPING SPREAD OF FIRE AND NOISE

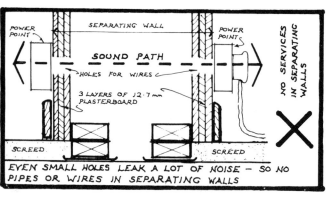

POWER POINT

SEPARATING WALL

POWER POINT

SOUND PATH

HOLES FOR WIRES

3 LAYERS OF 12·7mm PLASTERBOARD

NO SERVICES IN SEPARATING WALLS

SCREED

SCREED

EVEN SMALL HOLES LEAK A LOT OF NOISE — SO NO PIPES OR WIRES IN SEPARATING WALLS

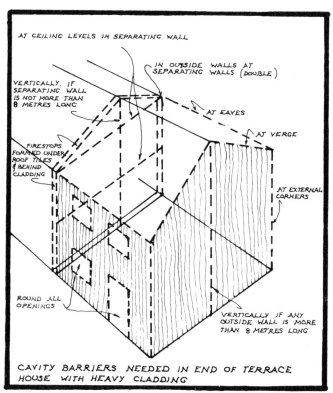

AT CEILING LEVELS IN SEPARATING WALL

IN OUTSIDE WALLS AT SEPARATING WALLS (DOUBLE)

VERTICALLY, IF SEPARATING WALL IS NOT MORE THAN 8 METRES LONG

AT EAVES

AT VERGE

FIRESTOPS FORMED UNDER ROOF TILES & BEHIND CLADDING

AT EXTERNAL CORNERS

ROUND ALL OPENINGS

VERTICALLY IF ANY OUTSIDE WALL IS MORE THAN 8 METRES LONG

CAVITY BARRIERS NEEDED IN END OF TERRACE HOUSE WITH HEAVY CLADDING

(i) External cladding

Lightweight cladding is carried on the timber structure. This can be in the form of tile hanging or horizontal timber boarding. This is usually carried on vertical battens fixed to outside wall panels. The vertical cavity behind the cladding allows moisture which gets behind the boarding to dry out. Details provide drainage and ventilation at lintels and ground level. Tile hanging is liable to get damaged on the ground storey but timber boarding is sufficiently robust.

Heavyweight cladding can be either brickwork or blockwork. This is carried directly off the foundations in the form of a single skin. Lintels, quite separate from those of the timber frames, are needed at openings.

A 50 mm cavity separates such cladding from the wall panels. This is detailed to drain outwards at lintels and at ground level. Changes in temperature and humidity may cause the timber frame and the cladding to move differentially. Clay brickwork has an initial expansion regardless of moisture and humidity conditions whilst concrete and calcium silicate (sand lime) bricks have a predominant shrinkage when drying.

The biggest movement is usually shrinkage of the timber frame when the dwelling first dries out. This can be as much as 10 mm or more at the eaves of a two-storey house, if the masonry leaf is built when the timber has a high moisture content because of damp site conditions.

So flexible wall ties are used across the cavity. Allowance for movement is also needed at eaves, verges and round windows and other openings. If forgotten, this relative movement can cause damage. But it can easily be allowed for on site.

Both types of cladding can, of course, be used together. For instance, brickwork is often used in vertical panels between openings. Lightweight cladding is used as infill above and below windows. This method avoids the need for lintels in the brickwork. Further, allowance for relative movement is needed only at roof level, above the brickwork panels.

4 Is preservative treatment of the timber needed?

Strictly speaking, it is not essential to treat all the softwood. Only with some pieces, such as base plates, is there a severe risk of fungal or insect attack. But full treatment is preferred by most private owners. So it is advisable to have the structural softwood treated throughout, including the trussed rafters.

Several suitable methods are available. They all require special plant, so treatment must be organised through the suppliers and cannot be done on site. Check with the supplier that the chemicals used are suitable for use with metal fittings.

Extra preservative should be available on site for brush application to all cuts, notches and holes made after treatment. This is most important for all the softwood in the outside walling, whether used for framing or cladding, especially at low level.

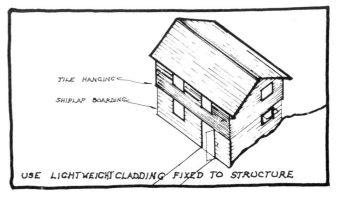

TILE HANGING
SHIPLAP BOARDING

USE LIGHTWEIGHT CLADDING FIXED TO STRUCTURE

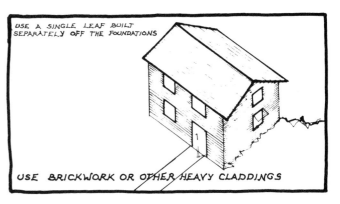

USE A SINGLE LEAF BUILT SEPARATELY OFF THE FOUNDATIONS

USE BRICKWORK OR OTHER HEAVY CLADDINGS

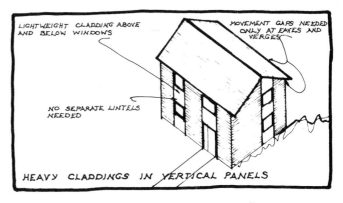

LIGHTWEIGHT CLADDING ABOVE AND BELOW WINDOWS

MOVEMENT GAPS NEEDED ONLY AT EAVES AND VERGES

NO SEPARATE LINTELS NEEDED

HEAVY CLADDINGS IN VERTICAL PANELS

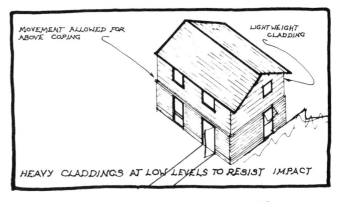

MOVEMENT ALLOWED FOR ABOVE COPING

LIGHTWEIGHT CLADDING

HEAVY CLADDINGS AT LOW LEVELS TO RESIST IMPACT

5 Must factory-made panels be used?

Since almost all timber frame houses in the UK are built using factory-made panels this Manual has been prepared with this method very much in mind. Any TRADA Regional Officer will be able to provide names of suitable suppliers to contact. They will need full information on what is required. (see chapters 2.2, 2.3 and 2.4).

But in countries where timber frame construction is traditional, the framing is frequently made up on site. This more often happens with small contracts, especially individual houses.

The NBA/TRADA Method is equally suitable for either method. Labour can be saved on site if arrangements can be made with the timber supplier for all the major pieces, such as studs and floor joists to be cut accurately to length before delivery. A clean level surface is needed on which to make up the panels, and if there is a foundation slab, this is quite suitable. Alternatively, panels can be made on long trestles. If identical panels are to be made, the first one can be made as a base and template for the others.

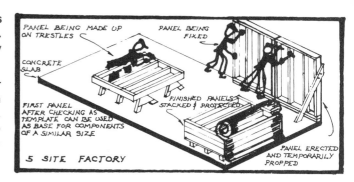

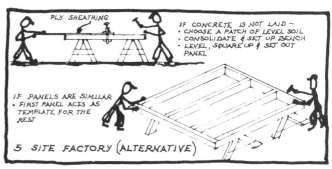

6 Must dimensional co-ordination be used?

Timber is a very adaptable building material. In traditional building, joists and rafters could always be cut to length on site, however inaccurate the brickwork. So, strictly speaking, dimensional co-ordination is not essential for timber frame construction, but throughout this Manual the structure is kept at 600 mm centres. Trussed rafters, floor joists and studs are always kept in line. This also means that best use is made of all the sheet materials fixed to the structure, as all are used in 1200 mm widths.

The Manual is also based on the use of dimensions which are multiples of 300 mm for the design of the dwelling on plan. Such systems have been used for many years in the public sector, and work well. It allows external joinery based on 300 mm multiples to be used. It reduces the quantity of useless off-cuts of sheet material. It simplifies the range of sizes for factory-made panels, and helps setting out on site.

The grid is used for setting out on plan the jambs of openings in external walls, and one face of internal partitions that carry floor joists. 300 mm multiples are used for the overall inside dimensions of dwellings, where 600 mm multiples are not suitable. Note that the basic thicknesses of separating walls between dwellings are as shown in the adjacent diagram and are increased where there are 'steps' and 'staggers'.

The heads of normal openings in outside walls are kept 2.100 m above finished floor level. If there is brick cladding, 75 mm per course is allowed, that is four courses per 300 mm, and the finished ground floor is lined up level with this coursing.

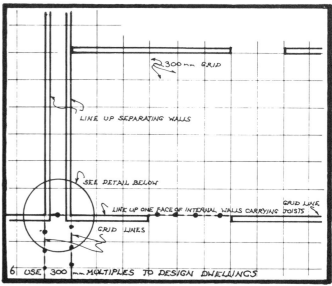

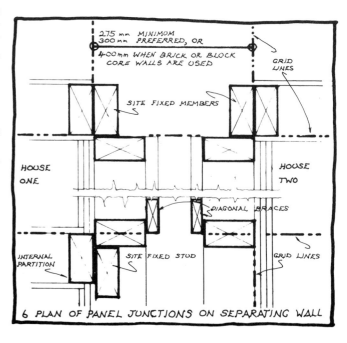

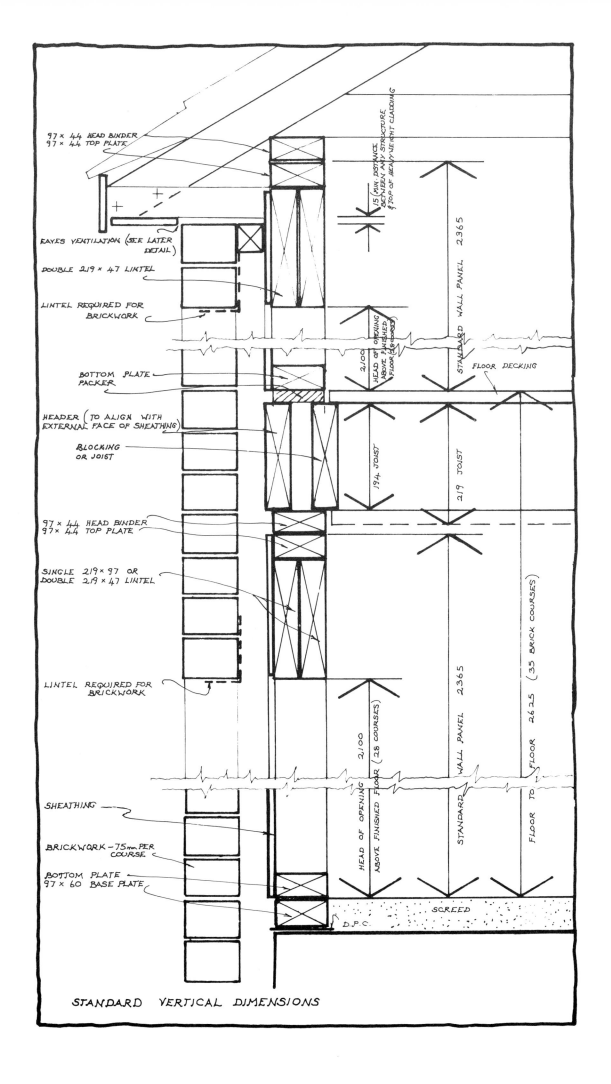

97 × 44 HEAD BINDER
97 × 44 TOP PLATE

EAVES VENTILATION (SEE LATER DETAIL)

DOUBLE 219 × 47 LINTEL

LINTEL REQUIRED FOR BRICKWORK

BOTTOM PLATE PACKER

HEADER (TO ALIGN WITH EXTERNAL FACE OF SHEATHING)

BLOCKING OR JOIST

97 × 44 HEAD BINDER
97 × 44 TOP PLATE

SINGLE 219 × 97 OR DOUBLE 219 × 47 LINTEL

LINTEL REQUIRED FOR BRICKWORK

SHEATHING

BRICKWORK – 75mm PER COURSE

BOTTOM PLATE
97 × 60 BASE PLATE

15 (MIN. DISTANCE BETWEEN ANY STRUCTURE & TOP OF HEAVYWEIGHT CLADDING

STANDARD WALL PANEL 2.365

HEAD OF OPENING ABOVE FINISHED FLOOR (36 COURSES)

2,100

FLOOR DECKING

194 JOIST

219 JOIST

HEAD OF OPENING 2,100 ABOVE FINISHED FLOOR (28 COURSES)

STANDARD WALL PANEL 2.365

FLOOR TO FLOOR 2,625 (35 BRICK COURSES)

SCREED

D.P.C.

STANDARD VERTICAL DIMENSIONS

9

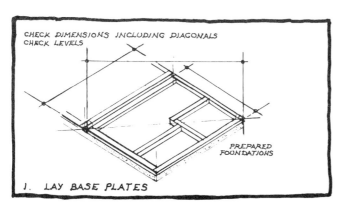

CHECK DIMENSIONS INCLUDING DIAGONALS
CHECK LEVELS

PREPARED FOUNDATIONS

1. LAY BASE PLATES

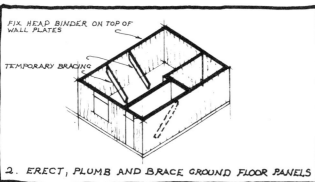

FIX HEAD BINDER ON TOP OF WALL PLATES

TEMPORARY BRACING

2. ERECT, PLUMB AND BRACE GROUND FLOOR PANELS

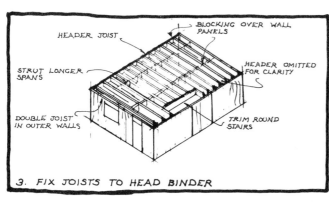

BLOCKING OVER WALL PANELS

HEADER JOIST

STRUT LONGER SPANS

HEADER OMITTED FOR CLARITY

DOUBLE JOIST IN OUTER WALLS

TRIM ROUND STAIRS

3. FIX JOISTS TO HEAD BINDER

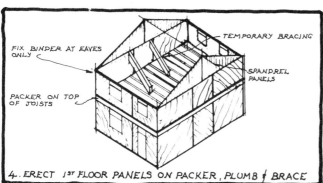

FIX BINDER AT EAVES ONLY

TEMPORARY BRACING

SPANDREL PANELS

PACKER ON TOP OF JOISTS

4. ERECT 1ST FLOOR PANELS ON PACKER, PLUMB & BRACE

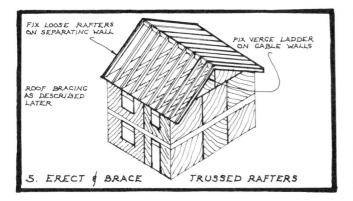

FIX LOOSE RAFTERS ON SEPARATING WALL

FIX VERGE LADDER ON GABLE WALLS

ROOF BRACING AS DESCRIBED LATER

5. ERECT & BRACE   TRUSSED RAFTERS

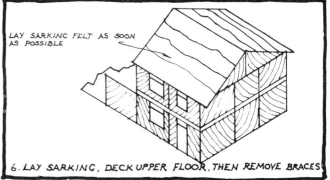

LAY SARKING FELT AS SOON AS POSSIBLE

6. LAY SARKING, DECK UPPER FLOOR, THEN REMOVE BRACES

7 How is the timber frame system erected?

To illustrate the principles, we describe here the erection of a two-storey house with solid concrete slab foundation. Base plates are first set out on foundation slab. They are laid on top of a DPC and bedded in mortar to the required level.

Great care is needed to ensure that they are not only in the correct position but also level, especially where factory-made panels are being used. This check must be made before fixing down takes place.

The wall panels of the ground floor are next erected and nailed down on to the base plates, extra pieces of timber being used at corners and junctions, as required. A head binder is then nailed on to the top plate of the wall panels. Temporary bracing is used, in case of high winds, and the wall frames are plumbed up as this is fixed.

The floor joists are then fixed to the head binder. These include a header joist on top of perimeter wall panels. Blockings are added between the joists as needed over wall panels to provide a bearing for the flooring, and a fixing for the ceiling lining.

Next a packer which corresponds to the flooring thickness is usually fixed round the perimeter of the dwelling. However if flooring of plywood with exterior glue is used it may be laid at this stage, being extended to occupy the space normally taken up by the packer.

This forms the seating for the first floor panels which are next erected and fixed. These include spandrel panels at gable ends and separating walls. A head binder is fixed on top of the external wall panels, which are then plumbed up and braced.

Finally the trussed rafters are erected and fixed, together with their bracing and verge ladders. Felt and battens are then laid over the trussed rafters.

This should be laid as soon as practicable in order to protect the timber, following which the upper floor decking can be laid if not already fixed.

Temporary bracing can then be removed.

8 Are there limits to the use of this Manual?

The structure of every timber frame house must be based on calculations and these can sometimes be quite complicated.

A simple, standard method is set out in this Manual. It includes a short set of tables and charts with which the structure can be designed. Used together, these obviate the need for detailed calculations.

It has been possible to do this only by setting limits to the dwelling design and siting. (Excluded are sites severely exposed to high winds). This does not mean that the timber frame method cannot be used outside the limits set. Such use, however, would call for specialist advice. If this is not readily available, your TRADA regional officer should be consulted (see inside back cover).

The basic scope of this Manual is for the design of dwellings within the following limitations:

(1)   one or two storeys;

(2)   detached, semi-detached or terraced;

(3)   simple rectangles on plan (except bungalows);

(4)   if the dwelling is of two storeys, no overhangs or set-backs at first floor level are permissible.

(5)   no gable wall or separating wall may be more than 10.200 metres long;

(6)   roofs must be covered with tiles and have symmetrical pitches between $22\frac{1}{2}°$ and $30°$ or $35°$ and $40°$.

Excluded are sites with exposure category 1 as defined in CP3 chapter V: part 2; 1972 (long stretches of open, level or near level country with no shelter) as well as sites which are exceptionally exposed (cliff tops, steeply sloping hillsides) for which specialist advice should be sought.

The rules of this Manual must be followed as regards:

(1)   the general specification of materials;

(2)   the standard details of construction;

(3)   keeping trussed rafters, floor joists and studs in line, set out at 600 mm centres;

(4)   the length of all wall frames, which must be from 1.800 to 3.600 metres;

(5)   openings in wall frames not to be more than 2.100 metres in length;

(6)   openings being kept at least 300 mm from the ends of frames, and from other openings;

(7)   using the standard heights for wall frames, storeys, and the heads of main openings;

(8)   using the standard method to ensure that dwellings will be stable in high winds;

(9)   the choice of lintels over openings;

(10) the sizing of floor joists;

(11) the use of one of the standard types of stairwell.

We repeat that to go outside these limits, or not to follow these design rules, *is* permissible, but *only on the advice of a structural engineer.*

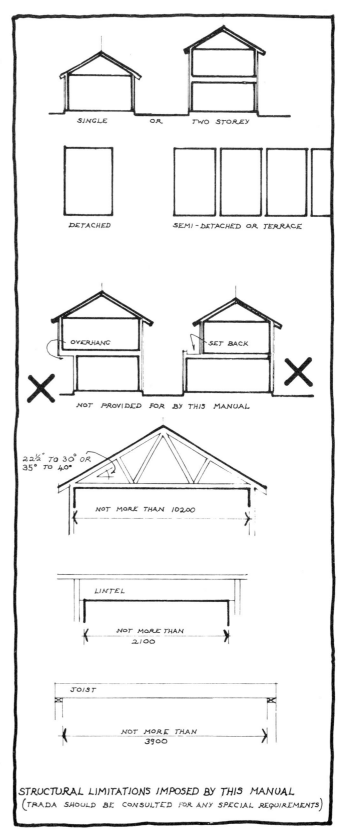

STRUCTURAL LIMITATIONS IMPOSED BY THIS MANUAL
(TRADA SHOULD BE CONSULTED FOR ANY SPECIAL REQUIREMENTS)

9 How does it meet building regulation requirements?

This is explained fully in Appendix 1 and, in the case of Scotland, Appendix 2. Regulations are liable to be amended as time goes on and it will be necessary to check that the method in this Manual still meets all the requirements.

Some regulations are open to slightly different interpretations. Not all of them are covered by deemed-to-satisfy specifications applicable to modern timber construction. Sometimes a building control officer will want to take account of local site or climatic conditions or particular combinations of construction before accepting all the details of a method such as this. If in doubt check with the local building inspector at an early stage on the acceptance of such matters as –

(a) ground cover beneath suspended timber ground floors;

(b) the positions of firestops in cavities between brick cladding and timber frames;

(c) requirements regarding non-combustible cladding and/or external fire resistance when external walls are built on or close to boundaries. 'There can be problems of interpretation when boundaries coincide with steps and staggers in separating walls.

In cases where there are problems of interpretation or the building control officer requires more back-up test information your TRADA regional officer will be pleased to help. He may be contacted at one of the addresses given on the inside back cover.

Work Below Ground Floor Level

In this section we deal only with work below ground floor level which is special to timber frame construction. In particular, problems of special foundations are beyond the scope of this Manual. But it is worth remembering that timber frame construction can offer two advantages on difficult sites.

First, it is possible to reduce the dead weight of dwellings, especially where lightweight cladding is used. Foundation costs can be reduced as a result on sites with low bearing capacity.

Second, timber frame dwellings are less liable than others to structural damage if there is serious settlement. They act as three dimensional structures, and resist cracking unlike brickwork. Timber frame construction can thus be used as an extra precaution on sites where ground movement is expected, such as with shrinkable clay or mining subsidence.

As with other methods of housebuilding, either solid concrete or suspended timber ground floors may be used.

Solid concrete ground floors

Edges of concrete slabs should be adequately supported from the foundations. Reinforcement should always be provided around the edges. Beneath any loadbearing walls, not built off independent foundations, reinforcement of the slab must be designed to transfer the loads on to adjacent foundations capable of carrying them.

Concrete ground floor slabs should not be used where a hardcore base more than 600 mm thick is needed, unless they are reinforced to span over the fill as a whole.

Where heavyweight cladding is used, this must be carried directly off the foundations.

60 × 97 mm softwood sections are used (63 × 100 mm processed) as base plates to carry the timber structure. They must be preservative treated and laid on dpc's. To obtain a true and level edge surface for fixing the wall panels, it is usually necessary to lay the dpc's on thin mortar beds. Plates are fixed with shot-fired or masonry nails at 300 mm centres penetrating through the dpc's at least 25 mm into the concrete slab. If the edge of the slab is faced with brick, which might be split by shot-fired masonry nails, the timber plate can be fixed with galvanised steel straps at 1200 mm centres bent over and nailed to the plates.

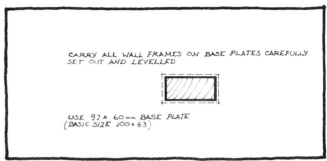

CARRY ALL WALL FRAMES ON BASE PLATES CAREFULLY SET OUT AND LEVELLED

USE 97 × 60 mm BASE PLATE (BASIC SIZE 100 × 63)

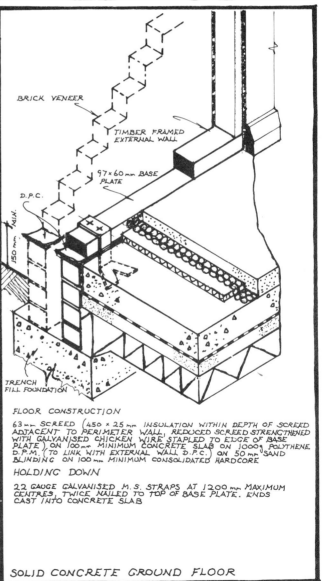

BRICK VENEER

TIMBER FRAMED EXTERNAL WALL

97 × 60 mm BASE PLATE

D.P.C.

150 mm MIN.

TRENCH FILL FOUNDATION

FLOOR CONSTRUCTION

63 mm SCREED (450 × 25 mm INSULATION WITHIN DEPTH OF SCREED ADJACENT TO PERIMETER WALL, REDUCED SCREED STRENGTHENED WITH GALVANISED CHICKEN WIRE STAPLED TO EDGE OF BASE PLATE) ON 100 mm MINIMUM CONCRETE SLAB ON 1000g POLYTHENE D.P.M. (TO LINK WITH EXTERNAL WALL D.P.C.) ON 50 mm SAND BLINDING ON 100 mm MINIMUM CONSOLIDATED HARDCORE

HOLDING DOWN

22 GAUGE GALVANISED M.S. STRAPS AT 1200 mm MAXIMUM CENTRES, TWICE NAILED TO TOP OF BASE PLATE. ENDS CAST INTO CONCRETE SLAB

SOLID CONCRETE GROUND FLOOR

The edge of the slab should always be protected with insulation to reduce heating costs. If a screed is used the floor edge should be insulated with expanded polystyrene or impregnated fibre insulation board in strips of 450 mm width and 25 mm overall thickness around the perimeter. This can be laid on top of the concrete slab if the screed is reinforced with galvanised chicken wire where its thickness is reduced to 35 mm by the edge insulation.

Alternatively a timber floating floor can be used. Then the insulation on which it is laid will extend to the timber plates around the perimeter and guard against edge heat losses. A 25 mm thick mineral fibre quilt should be used, fixed up around the edge of the floor. This will provide a gap to take up any possible expansion in the flooring in the future.

A damp-proof membrane will be required with solid concrete floors. This can be heavy duty polyethylene sheeting 0.24 mm thick (1000 g). If it is laid before the slab is cast, the hardcore base must be blinded with sand before the sheeting is laid, and plenty of time allowed for drying out of the slab. If the slab edge is faced with brick the polyethylene sheeting should be turned up behind the brick and lapped with the dpc beneath the timber plate.

Alternatively the dpm may be laid immediately below the screed where used, or the insulation on which 'floating' flooring of timber rests. The drying out period will be reduced in the first case and will be unnecessary in the second case. In both cases the polyethylene sheets must be lapped at least 300 mm at joints and lapped in with the dpc's beneath the timber plates.

Suspended timber ground floors

This method is usually best on made up or sloping sites where hardcore fill more than 600 mm thick would be needed under concrete slabs, which would have to be fully reinforced to span as a suspended floor.

Suspended floors are also being increasingly used on flat sites, because insulating quilt can easily be inserted between the joists to reduce heating costs. A further advantage is that the void under the joists can be used for electrical and plumbing runs. Suitable access and frost protection can be provided.

On relatively flat sites, where only shallow foundations are needed, short span floor joists are usually best, making use of occasional sleeper walls to give intermediate support.

Tendencies for this to cause summer overheating of the ground storey from solar gain through windows are unlikely to be significant since the Method limits the area of windows and other openings to a maximum of 40 per cent.

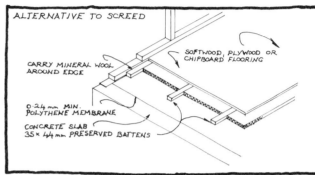

ALTERNATIVE TO SCREED

SOFTWOOD, PLYWOOD OR CHIPBOARD FLOORING

CARRY MINERAL WOOL AROUND EDGE

0.24 mm MIN. POLYTHENE MEMBRANE

CONCRETE SLAB

35 × 44 mm PRESERVED BATTENS

Chapter 2.1 contains a table giving a choice of suitable timber sections. On sites which require deeper foundations, or sites which are steeply sloping, it will usually be best to use longer spanning joists corresponding with room dimensions. The table provides for clear spans up to 3.900 m. Ground floor joist depths, as well as breadths, can be varied to suit different spans in the same house. This may involve notching some of them at the plate bearing positions. As long as the depths at the ends of joists are not reduced by more than 50 mm they will still be strong enough.

The sizes given for ground floor joists tend to be greater for a given span than those for upper floors. This is because they are designed to take a slightly higher superimposed load (of 2kN per m²) to ensure that they are not too 'springy' with more dynamic activities in the living spaces. It is important that this is understood by the people fixing the joists so that stronger ones are put in the right places.

Joists are carried on 97 × 60 mm plates (100 × 63 mm processed) laid on a dpc. The plates are fixed to the supporting walls with galvanised steel straps at 1800 mm centres. Joists are set out at 600 mm centres, with an extra joist under any lightweight partition parallel to the joists.

Note that in two-storey dwellings, any partition carrying upper floor joists must be supported directly by the foundations. At outside walls and separating walls parallel to the joists, a double joist is used. This is made up of two joists minimum 38 mm thick, spaced apart. At such walls at right angles to the joists, a 38 mm thick header joist is used. This is nailed to the joists. Over supporting sleeper walls, joists are butt jointed, and tied together with connector plates.

Blocking is fixed between joists over such supports. If through ventilation cannot be provided within the height of the sleeper wall, blockings should be a minimum of 25 mm less than the joist depth.

Blocking is also needed behind header joists if floor decking is not laid at the time of erecting the superstructure.

38 mm thick pieces are used for blocking, the same depth as the joists, and are offset, where necessary, so as to be able to support the floor decking.

Joists spanning more than 2.500 metres will require strutting at mid span. Either solid or herringbone strutting is suitable. For solid strutting, minimum 150 mm × 38 mm pieces are used.

Decking can be by any of the methods shown in this Manual as being suitable for upper floors. If desired a packer 97 mm wide and of the same thickness as the floor decking can be fixed to the top of the joists at the base of all wall frames. This allows the timber structure to be erected before the decking is laid. If decking is laid before the dwelling is protected from bad weather any underfloor insulation is liable to be damaged.

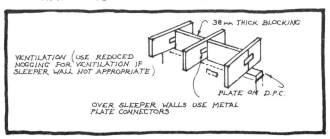

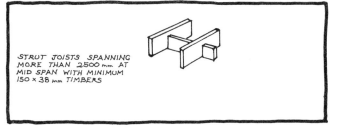

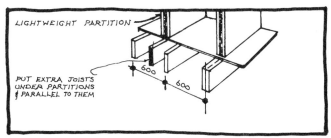

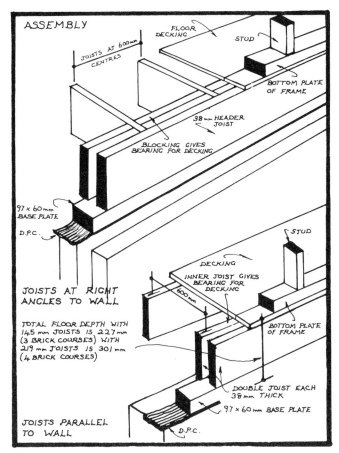

Ground cover beneath suspended timber floors

Suitable steps must be taken with suspended timber floors to protect the dwelling from rising moisture. The void under the floor must be back-filled as necessary, so that the finished level inside is not below the adjacent ground level outside.

The surface should then be blinded with sand. Heavy duty polyethylene 0.24 mm thick (1000 g) is then laid over the sand. Any laps should be at least 150 mm. The polyethylene is kept in position by spreading over it a blinding of weak concrete 50 mm thick.

Suitable steps are also essential to prevent any risk of fungal or insect attack on the softwood. Only preservative treated timber should be used below the ground floor decking. The bottom edge of all wall plates must be at least 75 mm above the top face of the concrete blinding.

The void under the suspended floor must be well ventilated. Internal sleeper wall construction must allow through ventilation. Well distributed air bricks in outside walls should provide at least 1500 mm² of clear opening per metre run of outside wall.

100 mm quilt is used to insulate the floor, laid immediately before the decking. The quilt is carried on stout netting dressed over the joists and stapled to them, before laying the insulation between the joists, ensuring that the top surface of the quilt is not in direct contact with the underside of the decking.

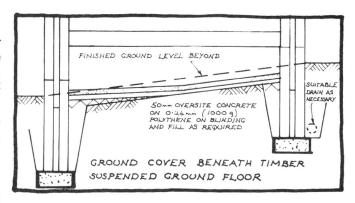

GROUND COVER BENEATH TIMBER SUSPENDED GROUND FLOOR

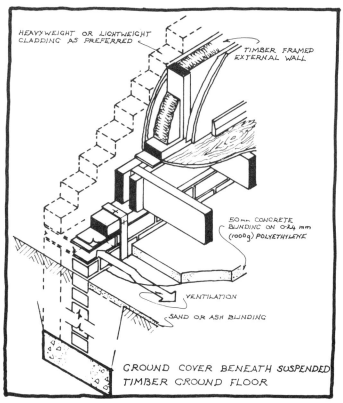

GROUND COVER BENEATH SUSPENDED TIMBER GROUND FLOOR

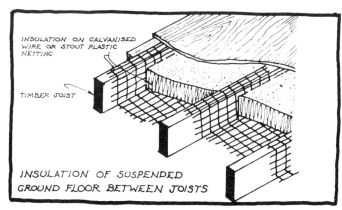

INSULATION OF SUSPENDED GROUND FLOOR BETWEEN JOISTS

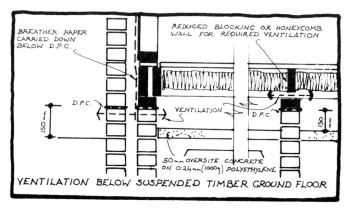

VENTILATION BELOW SUSPENDED TIMBER GROUND FLOOR

The Timber Structure

This part of the Manual deals in detail with the timber structure above finished ground floor level. The various parts are set out as follows:

(1) Wall frames, openings in wall frames, sheathing and bracing of frames, assembling the wall frames;

(2) Upper floors;

(3) Roof structure;

(4) Floor decking;

(5) Fixings.

1 Wall frames

A standard method is used for all wall frames. Wall frames are used for:

external walls;

separating walls, formed of double frames, one for each dwelling;

ground floor partitions that carry floor joists in two-storey dwellings;

internal wind-bracing partitions.

Note that any suitable lightweight method may be used for all other partitions. These are discussed further in Chapter 1.5.

A standard timber section is used for the wall frames. It is also used for additional pieces needed to assemble the structure, such as head binders and extra studs where frames meet at right angles.

The section used is 97 x 44 mm. This is processed, or machine-planed, out of 100 x 47 mm sawn timbers. Such processing is used throughout to help to keep the work accurate. Studs for external and internal wall panels are generally to be of General Structural Grade (GS). External wall studs for conditions of severe wind exposure have to be of Special Structural Grade (SS) where required in Chapter 2.1. Studs in non-loadbearing partitions do not have to be of stress graded timber.

Alternatively the finished section can be produced from 100 x 44 mm sawn timber by machining the opposite narrow faces down to a regular 97 mm dimension. This helps greatly when it comes to lining out the inside of the dwelling. For other details of softwood to be given when ordering see Chapter 2.3 on Materials.

If it is desired, as an alternative, to use Canadian surfaced timber, reference should be made to Appendix 3.

Frames without openings are made up with top and bottom plates, and studs at 600 mm centres. Simple butt joints are used. Studs must line up with any joists or trussed rafters carried by the frames. Each one must be over or within 40 mm of a stud.

For ease of handling no frame should be more than 3.600 metres long. End studs are set in so that the overall length of each frame is a multiple of 600 mm. The standard height of 2.365 m should be used. In the NBA/TRADA Method, this is fixed to suit brick courses of 75 mm.

Frames of outside walls and separating walls must not be less than 1.800 metres long. This helps with stability in high winds. The rule does not apply to any internal frames unless they are required to be sheathed.

(a) Openings in wall frames

Openings can be of any width up to a maximum of 2.100 m. The heads of all main openings should be 2.100 m above floor level. In all frames, any opening must be at least 300 mm away from the ends of the frame, and from any other opening.

Small openings which can be fitted between studs are simply framed up, using the standard section.

Larger openings require lintels. This includes openings in internal partitions carrying upper floor joists.

Lintels are always fitted between studs, directly under the head plate of the wall frame. They are carried on extra studs, known as cripple studs. Where pairs of cripple studs are shown as necessary, in Chapter 2.1, on both sides of an opening the lintel must bear on all of them.

In most cases two softwood pieces 219 × 47 mm can be used. This same section is used in the Method for floor joists. As with the joists, it has had the top and bottom edges machine planed. For further details of what to specify or order see Chapter 2.3 on Materials.

This standard lintel is used for all openings not more than 1.500 metres wide. It is also used for all openings up to 2.100 metres in frames in external walls that carry neither floor joists nor trussed rafters and may be used for lintel spans up to 2.100 metres when the lintel carries only floor loads, but check with Chapter 2.1 for grade of timber.

In other cases, a hardwood lintel is used up to a maximum span of 2.100 m.

'Staggered' openings should be avoided wherever possible. Otherwise, if the ground floor lintel is more than 1.500 metres wide, it will be necessary to have the lintel checked by a structural engineer.

One cripple stud at each end is usually enough to carry a lintel. But with wide openings and heavy loads, two cripple studs at each end may be needed, as shown in Chapter 2.1.

Where there is walling below the opening, this is made as part of the framed up panel. Short studs are set out at the normal 600 mm spacing.

If the frame is made off-site, a full-length bottom plate is used where there are doorways or other openings down to floor level. This prevents the frames from being twisted during handling. It also helps accurate erection. Only after erection is the bottom plate in the opening cut out.

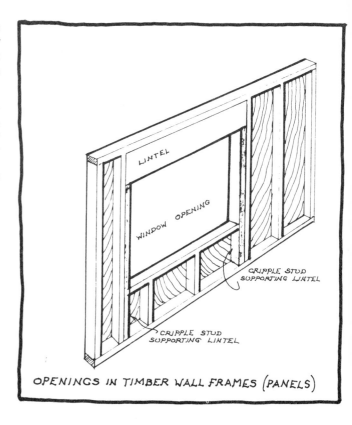

OPENINGS IN TIMBER WALL FRAMES (PANELS)

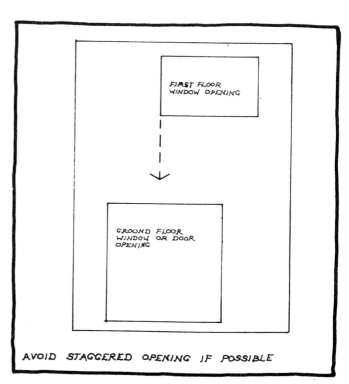

AVOID STAGGERED OPENING IF POSSIBLE

18

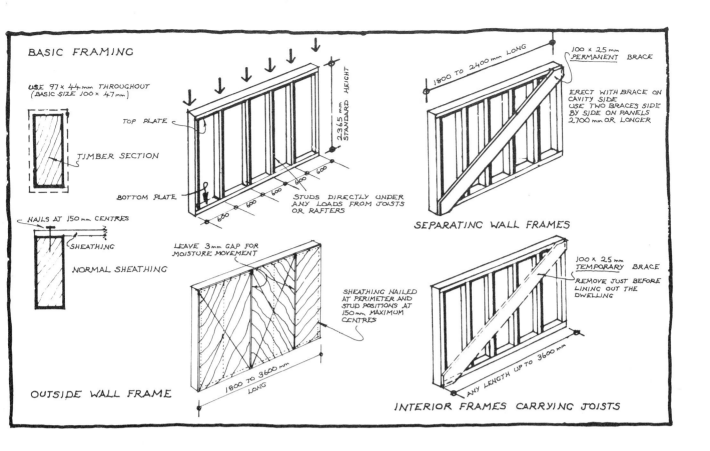

BASIC FRAMING

USE 97 x 44 mm THROUGHOUT
(BASIC SIZE 100 x 47 mm)

TIMBER SECTION

TOP PLATE

BOTTOM PLATE

STUDS DIRECTLY UNDER ANY LOADS FROM JOISTS OR RAFTERS

2365 mm STANDARD HEIGHT

600 600 600 600

NAILS AT 150 mm CENTRES

SHEATHING

NORMAL SHEATHING

LEAVE 3 mm GAP FOR MOISTURE MOVEMENT

SHEATHING NAILED AT PERIMETER AND STUD POSITIONS AT 150 mm MAXIMUM CENTRES

OUTSIDE WALL FRAME

1800 TO 3600 mm LONG

1800 TO 2400 mm LONG

100 x 25 mm PERMANENT BRACE

ERECT WITH BRACE ON CAVITY SIDE
USE TWO BRACES SIDE BY SIDE ON PANELS 2700 mm OR LONGER

SEPARATING WALL FRAMES

100 x 25 mm TEMPORARY BRACE

REMOVE JUST BEFORE LINING OUT THE DWELLING

ANY LENGTH UP TO 3600 mm

INTERIOR FRAMES CARRYING JOISTS

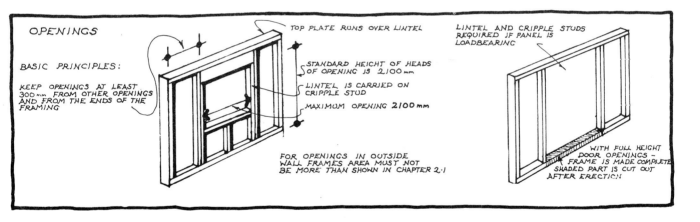

OPENINGS

BASIC PRINCIPLES:

KEEP OPENINGS AT LEAST 300 mm FROM OTHER OPENINGS AND FROM THE ENDS OF THE FRAMING

TOP PLATE RUNS OVER LINTEL

STANDARD HEIGHT OF HEADS OF OPENING IS 2100 mm

LINTEL IS CARRIED ON CRIPPLE STUD

MAXIMUM OPENING 2100 mm

FOR OPENINGS IN OUTSIDE WALL FRAMES AREA MUST NOT BE MORE THAN SHOWN IN CHAPTER 2.1

LINTEL AND CRIPPLE STUDS REQUIRED IF PANEL IS LOADBEARING

WITH FULL HEIGHT DOOR OPENINGS - FRAME IS MADE COMPLETE SHADED PART IS CUT OUT AFTER ERECTION

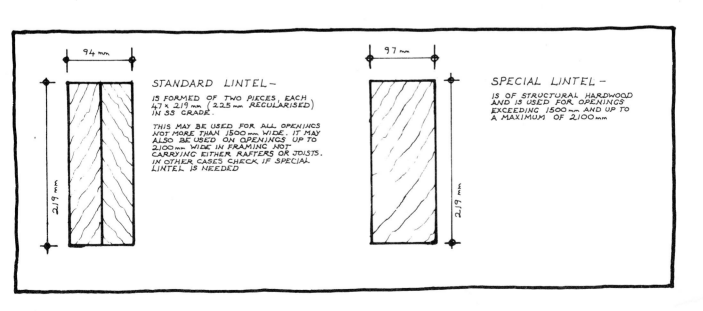

94 mm

219 mm

STANDARD LINTEL -

IS FORMED OF TWO PIECES, EACH 47 x 219 mm (225 mm REGULARISED) IN SS GRADE.

THIS MAY BE USED FOR ALL OPENINGS NOT MORE THAN 1500 mm WIDE. IT MAY ALSO BE USED ON OPENINGS UP TO 2100 mm WIDE IN FRAMING NOT CARRYING EITHER RAFTERS OR JOISTS. IN OTHER CASES CHECK IF SPECIAL LINTEL IS NEEDED

97 mm

219 mm

SPECIAL LINTEL -

IS OF STRUCTURAL HARDWOOD AND IS USED FOR OPENINGS EXCEEDING 1500 mm AND UP TO A MAXIMUM OF 2100 mm

(b) Sheathing and bracing

In the NBA/TRADA Method all outside wall panels are sheathed with plywood. For details of what to specify or order see Chapter 2.3 on Materials. Other materials may be used instead of plywood. Further details are given in Appendix III.

Sheathing must always be used in 1.200 metre widths, and to the full height of the panel. This is except for cutting round openings or at one end of a panel where the length is not a multiple of 1.200 metres.

Frames for separating walls have diagonal braces. 100 × 25 mm pieces are used, set out parallel to each other from opposite corners of the frame, one brace for panels up to 2400, two braces for panels 2700 to 3600.

In timber frame dwellings, wind loads are carried down to the foundation through the sheathed panels. Braced frames in separating walls act in the same way.

Every timber frame dwelling must be checked to ensure that there is enough sheathing and other bracing to take wind loads. The method to use is set out in this Manual in Chapter 2.1. This check must be made before finalising the design and layout of the dwelling.

(c) Assembling the wall frames

At external corners, two extra pieces of the standard wall frame section are used. This includes corners between outside walls and separating walls. These form a corner post. Loadbearing and windbracing internal partitions are also assembled with the outside wall panels using extra studs, at the junctions.

In separating walls, the two frames (one for each dwelling) are set apart to give an overall width of 300 mm. They are connected together using 40 mm × 3 mm flat galvanised steel straps. These are fixed at ceiling level to alternate studs. This is done on both floors in two-storey dwellings, and is enough to tie together the two dwellings whilst giving only a very limited path for the spread of noise.

The wall frames are tied together at the top by nailing on an extra piece of the standard section. This is known as a head binder. It is used throughout on the top of all wall panels, except at ceiling level at gable ends and separating walls, where there are spandrel frames. These effectively tie the wall frames together, so no head binder is needed in this position.

A packer corresponding with the flooring thickness is normally used at the base of all wall frames carried on floor joists.

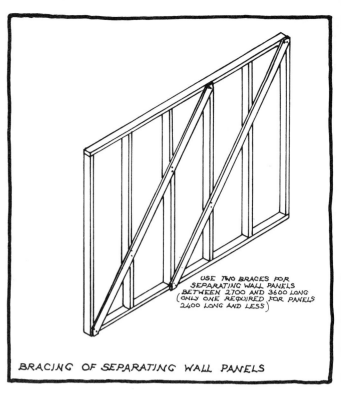

USE TWO BRACES FOR SEPARATING WALL PANELS BETWEEN 2700 AND 3600 LONG (ONLY ONE REQUIRED FOR PANELS 2400 LONG AND LESS)

BRACING OF SEPARATING WALL PANELS

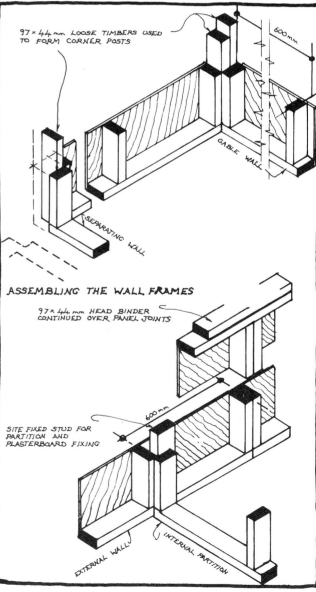

97 × 44 mm LOOSE TIMBERS USED TO FORM CORNER POSTS

600 mm

GABLE WALL

SEPARATING WALL

ASSEMBLING THE WALL FRAMES

97 × 44 mm HEAD BINDER CONTINUED OVER PANEL JOINTS

SITE FIXED STUD FOR PARTITION AND PLASTERBOARD FIXING

600 mm

EXTERNAL WALL

INTERNAL PARTITION

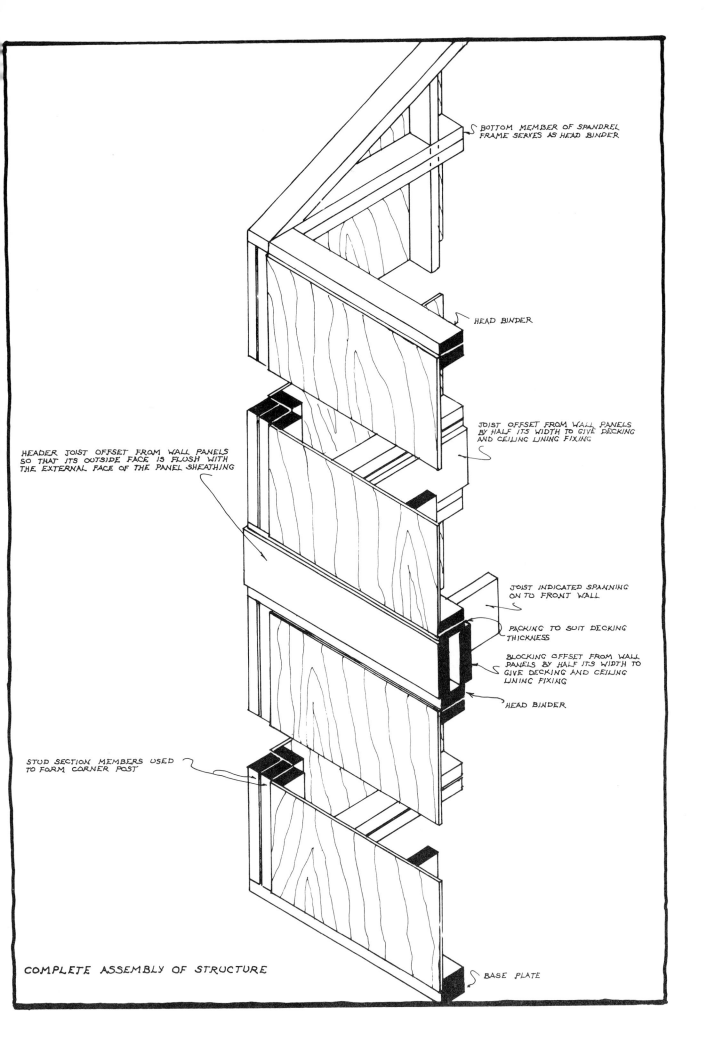

BOTTOM MEMBER OF SPANDREL FRAME SERVES AS HEAD BINDER

HEAD BINDER

JOIST OFFSET FROM WALL PANELS BY HALF ITS WIDTH TO GIVE DECKING AND CEILING LINING FIXING

HEADER JOIST OFFSET FROM WALL PANELS SO THAT ITS OUTSIDE FACE IS FLUSH WITH THE EXTERNAL FACE OF THE PANEL SHEATHING

JOIST INDICATED SPANNING ON TO FRONT WALL

PACKING TO SUIT DECKING THICKNESS

BLOCKING OFFSET FROM WALL PANELS BY HALF ITS WIDTH TO GIVE DECKING AND CEILING LINING FIXING

HEAD BINDER

STUD SECTION MEMBERS USED TO FORM CORNER POST

COMPLETE ASSEMBLY OF STRUCTURE

BASE PLATE

21

2 Upper floors

Upper floor joists are always used at 600 mm spacings in the NBA/TRADA Method. Two types are used:

194 mm deep joists in General Structural Grade (GS). These are regularised from 200 mm timbers (machine planed on both edges).

219 mm deep joists in Special Structural Grade (SS). These are regularised from 225 mm timbers; the same material is used for lintels. These joists are notched at each end to reduce the depth to 194 mm.

If 219 mm deep joists are used with 194 mm in the same dwelling the changeover may happen only at partitions. Any change of ceiling level inside a room is thus avoided.

The span tables in Chapter 2.1 of this Manual are used to size the joists, and find the breadths required.

The span tables allow for normal loading by lightweight partitions at right angles to the joists.

An extra joist must be added where there are partitions parallel to the joists, though short lengths of partition less than 600 mm long may be ignored.

At outside walls and separating walls the framing is completed by an extra joist of minimum 194 × 38 mm section. This is known as a header joist when at right angles to the floor joists. At external walls the outer or header joist is offset to the line of the outside face of the wall panel sheathing.

A double joist is used where the wall is parallel to the joists. The inner joist is offset so as to be able to carry the ceiling plasterboard, and upper floor decking.

Over partitions carrying them, joists are butt jointed, tied together with connector plates and given equal bearing on the timber plate. Blocking is fixed between joists over such partitions. Blocking is also used between joists behind header joists. Such blocking is offset so as to be able to carry floor decking and plasterboard.

At junctions with separating walls the blocking also acts as additional fire protection to the header joist and must therefore be tightly fitted.

Joists spanning 2.500 m or more will require strutting at mid span. Either solid or herringbone strutting is suitable. For solid strutting minimum 150 mm × 38 mm pieces are used.

A straight flight stair will need a clear opening about 2600 long. This can usually be either between load-bearing frames or on one side of a stairwell 1.800 metres wide. The trimmer sizes required are indicated in Chapter 2.1.

A dog-legged stair requires a clear opening about 2.100 metres by 1.800 metres. This can either be directly between wall frames or in a stairwell about 3.000 metres wide. The trimmer sizes needed are shown in Chapter 2.1.

Note that the sizes shown are suitable only if joist hangers are used to carry trimmed joists and trimmers. There must be no cutting or notching. For other designs, and larger openings, trimmers and trimming joists will need to be calculated in the usual way and any effects on overall stability considered.

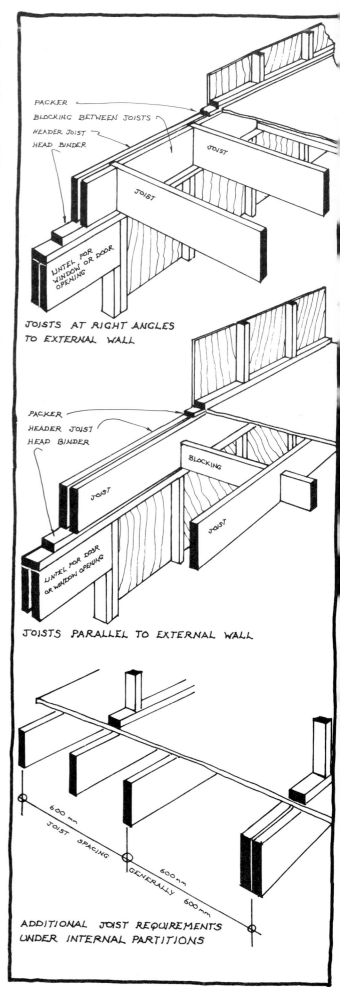

JOISTS AT RIGHT ANGLES TO EXTERNAL WALL

JOISTS PARALLEL TO EXTERNAL WALL

ADDITIONAL JOIST REQUIREMENTS UNDER INTERNAL PARTITIONS

Trimming round stairwells is carried out as in other housing, but avoiding long trimming joists spanning over ground floor rooms. They must be specially calculated, and usually require heavy and expensive sections. They must also be carried on extra studs in the wall frames.

The following designs will cover most cases. The NBA/TRADA Manual uses a basic floor to floor height of 2625 mm. This is 35 courses of brickwork, using 75 mm per course.

Stairs can have 13 risers, each about 202 mm. Twelve treads, each with a going of 225 mm, are suitable. The rules of thumb below assume these sizes. Such stairs can be either straight flight or dog-legged.

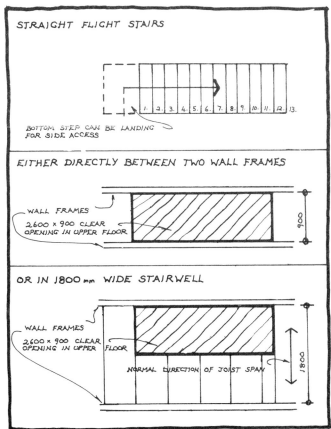

STRAIGHT FLIGHT STAIRS

BOTTOM STEP CAN BE LANDING FOR SIDE ACCESS

EITHER DIRECTLY BETWEEN TWO WALL FRAMES

WALL FRAMES

2600 × 900 CLEAR OPENING IN UPPER FLOOR

900

OR IN 1800 mm WIDE STAIRWELL

WALL FRAMES

2600 × 900 CLEAR OPENING IN UPPER FLOOR

NORMAL DIRECTION OF JOIST SPAN

1800

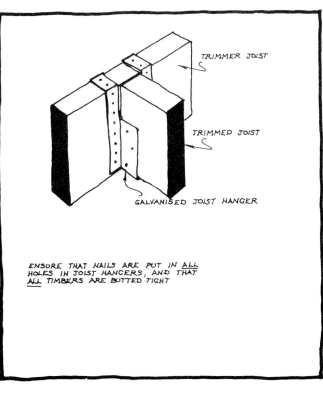

TRIMMER JOIST

TRIMMED JOIST

GALVANISED JOIST HANGER

ENSURE THAT NAILS ARE PUT IN ALL HOLES IN JOIST HANGERS, AND THAT ALL TIMBERS ARE BUTTED TIGHT

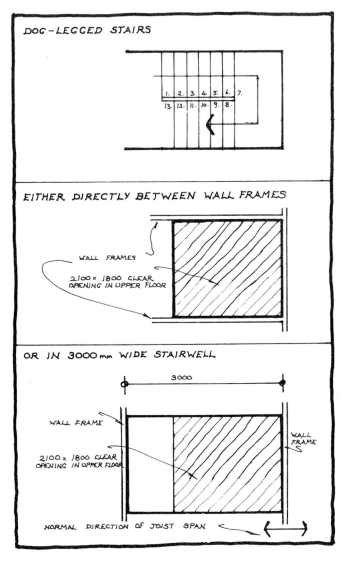

DOG-LEGGED STAIRS

EITHER DIRECTLY BETWEEN WALL FRAMES

WALL FRAMES

2100 × 1800 CLEAR OPENING IN UPPER FLOOR

OR IN 3000 mm WIDE STAIRWELL

3000

WALL FRAME

2100 × 1800 CLEAR OPENING IN UPPER FLOOR

WALL FRAME

NORMAL DIRECTION OF JOIST SPAN

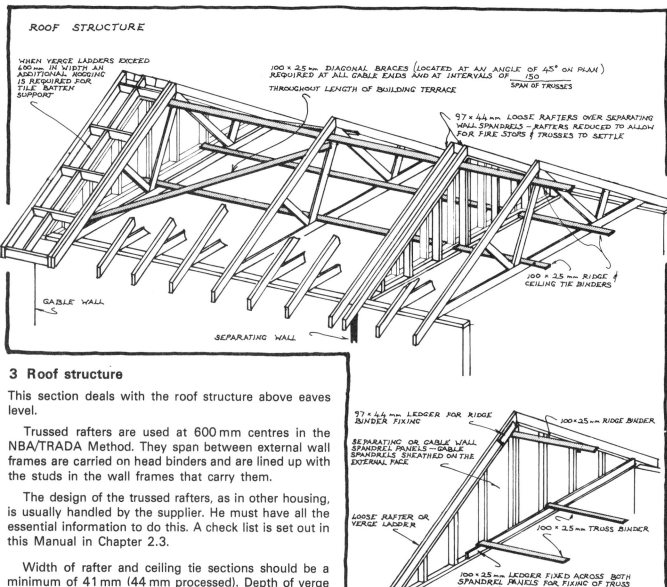

ROOF STRUCTURE

WHEN VERGE LADDERS EXCEED 600mm IN WIDTH AN ADDITIONAL NOGGING IS REQUIRED FOR TILE BATTEN SUPPORT

100 x 25 mm DIAGONAL BRACES (LOCATED AT AN ANGLE OF 45° ON PLAN) REQUIRED AT ALL GABLE ENDS AND AT INTERVALS OF $\frac{150}{\text{SPAN OF TRUSSES}}$ THROUGHOUT LENGTH OF BUILDING TERRACE

97 x 44 mm LOOSE RAFTERS OVER SEPARATING WALL SPANDRELS — RAFTERS REDUCED TO ALLOW FOR FIRE STOPS & TRUSSES TO SETTLE

100 x 25 mm RIDGE & CEILING TIE BINDERS

GABLE WALL

SEPARATING WALL

97 x 44 mm LEDGER FOR RIDGE BINDER FIXING

100 x 25 mm RIDGE BINDER

SEPARATING OR GABLE WALL SPANDREL PANELS — GABLE SPANDRELS SHEATHED ON THE EXTERNAL FACE

LOOSE RAFTER OR VERGE LADDER

100 x 25 mm TRUSS BINDER

100 x 25 mm LEDGER FIXED ACROSS BOTH SPANDREL PANELS FOR FIXING OF TRUSS BINDERS & CEILING PLASTERBOARD

3 Roof structure

This section deals with the roof structure above eaves level.

Trussed rafters are used at 600 mm centres in the NBA/TRADA Method. They span between external wall frames are carried on head binders and are lined up with the studs in the wall frames that carry them.

The design of the trussed rafters, as in other housing, is usually handled by the supplier. He must have all the essential information to do this. A check list is set out in this Manual in Chapter 2.3.

Width of rafter and ceiling tie sections should be a minimum of 41 mm (44 mm processed). Depth of verge ladder and loose rafter sections used elsewhere in the roof must be compatible with the selected rafter depth of the trusses.

The structure above eaves at gables is completed with spandrel frames. The same frame size is used for both gable ends and separating walls. 97 mm × 44 mm framing is used as elsewhere, with vertical studs at 600 mm centres. Spandrel frames for outside walls are sheathed.

No sheathing is needed in separating walls. Spandrel frames are fixed directly on to the wall frames. No head binder is needed. The bottom plates of spandrel frames tie together the wall frames that carry them.

At gable ends, verge ladders are used. These are made up out of 44 mm framing with a depth to suit that of the trussed rafters. Blocking is used over the wall frame carrying verge ladders. The design of verge ladder in this Manual is suitable for widths up to 1.200 metres. This is the total width of the ladder, and provides a maximum projection of 500 mm from the face of the timber structure.

When verge ladders exceed 600 mm in width, addi-

tional noggings are required for supporting tile battens. These are located above the spandrel frames.

At separating walls, loose rafters are used fixed to the top plates of the spandrel frames.

Verge ladders to gable walls and rafters to separating walls are fixed after the trussed rafters, to line up with them as they will be when carrying the weight of the roofing. The truss manufacturer should be asked for information on the apex deflection of trusses when they are carrying the deadweight of the tiles and ceiling. The depth of loose rafters at separating walls and the setting out of spandrel frames must also allow for the thickness of the asbestos insulation board or equivalent.

Note that in Chapter 2.3 it is recommended that trussed rafters be made slightly oversize. This allows for lining up at each end by packing the verge ladders or loose rafters.

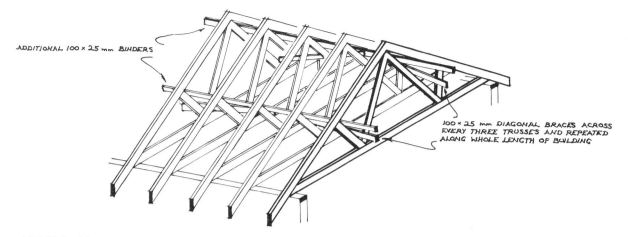

ADDITIONAL 100 x 25 mm BINDERS

100 x 25 mm DIAGONAL BRACES ACROSS
EVERY THREE TRUSSES AND REPEATED
ALONG WHOLE LENGTH OF BUILDING

ADDITIONAL ROOF BRACING REQUIREMENTS WHERE TRUSS SPANS EXCEED 7·800 METRES

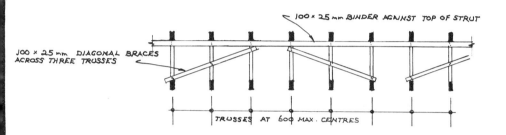

100 x 25 mm BINDER AGAINST TOP OF STRUT

100 x 25 mm DIAGONAL BRACES
ACROSS THREE TRUSSES

TRUSSES AT 600 MAX. CENTRES

ELEVATION OF ADDITIONAL BRACING REQUIREMENTS

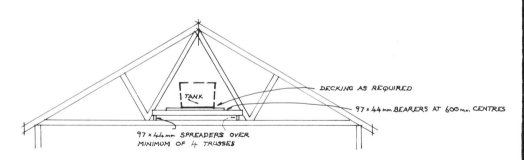

DECKING AS REQUIRED

97 x 44 mm BEARERS AT 600 mm CENTRES

TANK

97 x 44 mm SPREADERS OVER
MINIMUM OF 4 TRUSSES

TANK PLATFORM

Verge ladders and rafters for separating walls need to be delivered slightly over-length, then cut to length after fixing to line up with the ends of the trussed rafters.

100 x 25 mm ceiling ledgers are fixed to the inside face of the spandrel panels. These are needed for fixing plasterboard ceilings, as well as for fixing bracing. The roof structure is then braced. This ties together all the trussed rafters and the spandrel panels.

Bracing is carried out using 100 mm x 25 mm pieces. This is twice nailed to every trussed rafter, using 75 mm nails. If such braces are in two pieces, then these must be lapped over at least two trussed rafters.

The bracing needed is as follows:

a full length binder under the ridge;

two full length binders fixed on top of the ceiling ties;

diagonal bracing fixed to the underside of rafters.

If trussed rafters span more than 7.800 m, extra bracing will be needed, as shown in the diagram.

The roof structure is completed by laying and fixing the sarking felt straight away, to protect the timber structure, using occasional temporary battens if the fixing of the tiling battens has to be done later.

Where cold water storage tanks occur in the roof space the weight should be distributed evenly to the roof trusses as shown in the diagram.

4 Floor decking

Floor decking can be laid as the superstructure is erected or as soon as the sarking felt is in position to assist in bracing up the structure.

Any of the following may be used:

21 mm tongued and grooved softwood boarding;

22 mm flooring grade chipboard tongued and grooved on all edges;

19 mm plywood tongued and grooved on long edges.

If the decking is going to be exposed to the elements before the structure is roofed, every endeavour should be made to keep it as dry as possible and only exterior quality ply or moisture resistant chipboard should be used.

For further details of what to specify or order see Chapter 2.3.

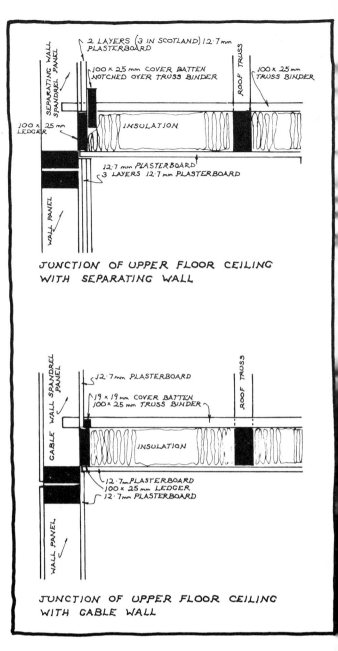

JUNCTION OF UPPER FLOOR CEILING WITH SEPARATING WALL

JUNCTION OF UPPER FLOOR CEILING WITH GABLE WALL

Where sheet materials are used, any free edges not directly on the joists must be properly supported 44 x 44 mm noggings should be fixed under any unsupported edges which are not tongued and grooved. Plywood is always laid with the face grain at right angles to the joists. Chipboard sheets should also be laid with the long edges at right angles to the joists.

5 Fixings

Do not forget that the stability of the structure will depend upon the various pieces being well fixed together. Site inspection is essential before the structure is covered by breather paper, insulation and plasterboard linings. For general assembly, normal round plain head nails to BS 1202: Part 1: 1974, with bright finish are used.

The range of nails needed, and the diameter of each, is as follows:

Length in mm	Diameter in mm	Approximate SWG
100	4.0	8
75	3.75	9
50	3.0	11

These nails are used as follows:

(1) At all butt joints between two pieces at right angles (except only when trimming joists round stairs):

Two 100 mm nails, end nailed – or three 75 mm nails, skew nailed.

Skew nailing is used only where end nailing is not practicable, for instance when fixing blocking to joists.

(2) Where any two pieces are placed together parallel to each other, horizontally, vertically, or along the slope of the roof.

75 mm nails at 300 mm centres.

Where there is access from both sides, for instance when nailing together two pieces to form the standard lintel, or the end studs of two wall frames, nailing is done alternately from opposite sides.

In some cases it may be necessary to skew nail, for instance when fixing down header joists to head binders.

(3) Sheathing to wall frames

50 mm nails at 150 mm centres to all frame members.

(4) Fixing down ends of trussed rafters and floor joists, as well as rungs of verge ladders to the top plate of wall framing.

Three 100 mm nails, skew nailed (or proprietary connector).

(5) Fixing bracing on to wall frames in separating walls into every stud. Also fixing bracing to trussed rafters, into every trussed rafter.

Two 75 mm nails.

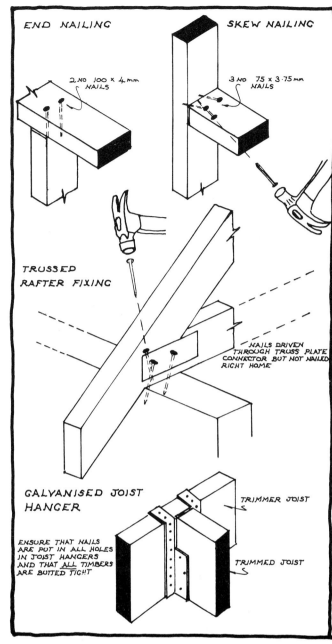

END NAILING — 2 NO 100 x 4mm NAILS

SKEW NAILING — 3 NO 75 x 3.75mm NAILS

TRUSSED RAFTER FIXING — NAILS DRIVEN THROUGH TRUSS PLATE CONNECTOR BUT NOT NAILED RIGHT HOME

GALVANISED JOIST HANGER — ENSURE THAT NAILS ARE PUT IN ALL HOLES IN JOIST HANGERS AND THAT ALL TIMBERS ARE BUTTED TIGHT — TRIMMER JOIST — TRIMMED JOIST

Special fixings are required as follows:

(1) Trimming round stairs.

Galvanised joist hangers are used with straps that are dressed over the top edge of the joist carrying the cut end. To be fixed according to manufacturer's instructions.

(2) Connecting floor joists where ends are butted together over wall plates or head binders.

One 18g 200 mm by 50 mm galvanised steel plate. Fix with three 50 mm nails into each joist.

(3) Connecting the two wall frames in separating walls. A connection is needed at 1200 mm centres at each ceiling level.

One 18g 200 mm by 50 mm galvanised steel plate. Fix at each end to studs with three 50 mm nails.

(4) Fixing down base plate and wall plates to foundations.

Use either masonry nails or shot fired nails at 300 mm centres used in accordance with manufacturer's instructions. Nails must penetrate at least 25 mm into concrete. Or 25 mm x 16g galvanised mild steel straps at 1200 mm centres — twice nailed to base plates with 50 mm nails. Strap taken down minimum 4 courses and turned into brickwork, or to have fish-tail end and cast into slabs.

Heating, Plumbing and Electrical Installations

In this chapter, we explain how best the various services can be installed in dwellings built in accordance with this Manual.

Sequence of building

Work can start on these services as soon as the dwelling is protected by the sarking felt.

Chimneys, flues and vent pipes that pass through the roof should be carried out without delay. This will then allow the dwelling to be ready for tilers as soon as possible.

All the runs of piping and wiring carried within the structure must, of course, be completed before lining out starts.

Fitting in general wiring and pipework

For general wiring, drilled holes in wall frames and floor joists are used. The holes must be drilled at the centre of the section and be no bigger than 30 mm diameter. Holes are to be kept at least 300 mm away from the ends of studs, joists and other structural pieces, and from any other hole.

Notches are only allowed in joists and the following rules must be followed:

(1) All notches to be in top edge of joist. (This may involve fixing some pipework before floor laying);

(2) No notches nearer to supporting plate than one-tenth joist span;

(3) No notches further from supporting plate than one-fifth joist span;

(4) Maximum depth of notch in 194 mm joist – 29 mm;

(5) Maximum depth of notch in 219 mm joist – 32 mm.

There must be no drilling or cutting of trussed rafters. No wiring or pipework should be placed in separating walls. This is because they would require holes in the plasterboard linings. These would tend to allow noise through from one dwelling to the next.

Special provision for wiring will be needed as a result along separating walls, at ground floor level of dwellings with concrete slab foundations.

In some cases it may be necessary to carry services in the screed. In others, for example in kitchens, it may be best to provide a surface-mounted duct.

As far as possible, pipework in external walls should be

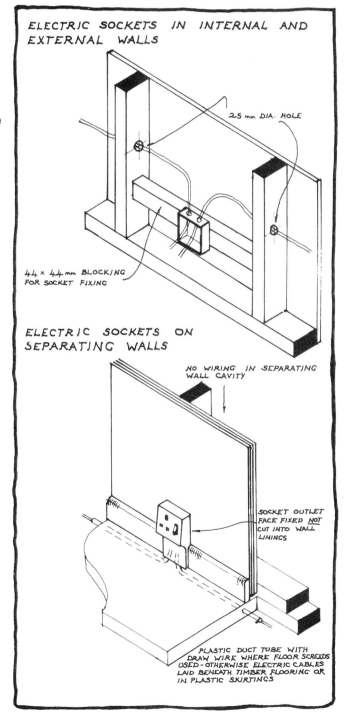

ELECTRIC SOCKETS IN INTERNAL AND EXTERNAL WALLS

25 mm DIA. HOLE

44 × 44 mm BLOCKING FOR SOCKET FIXING

ELECTRIC SOCKETS ON SEPARATING WALLS

NO WIRING IN SEPARATING WALL CAVITY

SOCKET OUTLET FACE FIXED NOT CUT INTO WALL LININGS

PLASTIC DUCT TUBE WITH DRAW WIRE WHERE FLOOR SCREEDS USED - OTHERWISE ELECTRIC CABLES LAID BENEATH TIMBER FLOORING OR IN PLASTIC SKIRTINGS

avoided. If such runs are necessary, then they must be adequately lagged by the plumbers, and the insulation quilt must be tucked between them and the sheathing.

Boxes for power points and switches should be securely mounted on blocking pieces fixed between studs before lining out. 44 x 44 mm pieces are suitable.

WC and bath connections to stack pipes are to be kept above the decking on the upper floors. In particular, plumbers should not cut or notch joists in making such connections.

Selection of heating systems

To get the best out of timber frame construction, full account should be taken of two important features. First, the amount of heat that has to be introduced is much less than with normal construction. Second, the structure will warm up quickly and lends itself to economies from intermittent heating systems, compared with ones that feed heat into the whole house on a 24 hour basis.

By careful choice of a low capacity quick response system, it is possible to reduce both initial installation costs and running costs for occupants.

Chimneys for solid fuel and gas appliances

Such chimneys can be carried out in insulated metal units. These can be erected quickly, and supported off the timber framing. The units must conform to BS 4543. The manufacturer will indicate what distance such units must be kept from floor joists, decking, trussed rafters, tiling battens, and any other combustible materials. This clearance is usually from 40 mm to 50 mm.

This same clearance must be provided round the units throughout at first floor level in two storey dwellings, where they must be cased in. Such casing is needed even if the chimney passes through a cupboard or store.

There should be access to such chimneys for their entire length. It must be possible to inspect them from time to time and, if necessary, replace them at a later date. So casings must be removable.

Manufacturers will supply the necessary steel plates to ensure that there is fire-stopping round the units at upper floor and ceiling levels. Such plates usually act also as supports. They can be screwed to bearers fixed between the floor joists.

Manufacturers will usually also supply such fittings as access plates for cleaning, supports to bracket the chimneys off rafters, and preformed flashings for the roof.

Alternatively, a chimney can be built as an independent structure. It can be stabilised by being linked to the timber structure. Metal ties must maintain a gap of 38 mm between the timber and the face of the chimney. Tie ends must be kept at least 50 mm from the inner flue surface.

A chimney or fireplace may be positioned against a separating wall but not built into it. The complete timber framed wall, including all layers of plasterboard, must be continued behind it. Remember to allow for small vertical movements in detailing the flashing between the upper chimney and roofing. The Solid Fuel Advisory Service can offer expert advice on solid fuel systems and chimneys.

Gas appliances with balanced flues

Gas appliances are increasingly designed to be used with balanced flues, mounted on outside walls.

Such flues usually consist of an outlet for the exhaust gases and an outer metal casing. The space between the

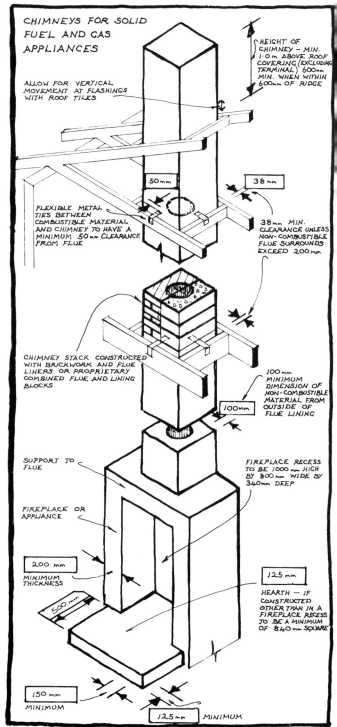

two forms the air inlet. The appliance is thus room-sealed.

Care must be taken with the positioning of balanced flue outlets, especially when in recesses or near windows, eaves or other projections. Appliance manufacturers or area gas boards should be consulted if in doubt.

With some appliances, it is necessary to keep them at least 75 mm away from any combustible material, or to provide a shield of non-combustible material at least 25 mm thick. Many appliances are, however, designed so that no such precaution is necessary.

It is usually sufficient to keep combustible materials at least 50 mm away from the exhaust flue. Sheathing and any timber cladding should be cut to suit. Cavities round the flue are closed with 50 mm mineral wool blanket, wire reinforced. The precise details needed will depend upon the design of the appliance. Manufacturers and area gas boards will give further help.

Finishing off the Roof

Any normal type of tile may be used. Note that if lightweight roofing is being considered, then specialist advice will be needed to check that the dwelling is still stable in high winds. The standard method of calculation must not be used if the weight of the roof covering differs from the following:

(1) $22\frac{1}{2}°$ to 30° roof pitches – 45 to 55 kg/m²;
(2)   35° to 40° roof pitches – 70 to 80 kg/m².

Normal roofings are used as in other housing, so we deal here only with the special needs of timber frame construction in finishing off the roof.

When to lay tiles

In timber frame construction the roof finish is laid as soon as possible after the structure is complete. This is to give permanent protection to the inside of the dwelling, so that finishing can proceed.

In two storey houses, the upper floor should be decked or temporarily braced to provide stability whilst tiling. Any flues and vent pipes must of course be fixed first, before the tiling.

If there is only lightweight cladding under eaves and verges, then these can be carried out in the normal way, before tiles are laid, but with heavyweight cladding, special care is needed. Verges and eaves must be carried only on the roof structure. A gap for vertical movement of 15 mm must be left between the roof structure and the top of the heavyweight cladding at eaves and verges. This will include any soffit boards applied to the underside of eaves and verges. No part of the eaves or verges should be fixed to the heavyweight cladding.

Eaves and verges must also be designed to allow brick-layers to carry out the top few courses without difficulty. Special steps may well be needed with narrow or 'clipped' eaves and verges.

An example of how this can be done is shown, where there are clipped eaves. Shiplap boarding is used instead of a single eaves board. The top board only is fixed before the tilers arrive. The remaining boards are fixed after the bricklayers have finished.

As with other housing, there must be fire stopping under tiles at separating walls. The tiles must be well bedded on compressed mineral wool and a 10 mm asbestos insulation board or equivalent firestop is included over separating wall rafters and under the sarking felt.

Also as with other housing, boxed-in eaves will need cavity barriers at the separating wall. The mineral wool quilt used elsewhere in the separating wall will be suitable.

Eaves must be designed to allow the roof space to be well ventilated. The total free area should be not less than one three hundredth of the roof space area.

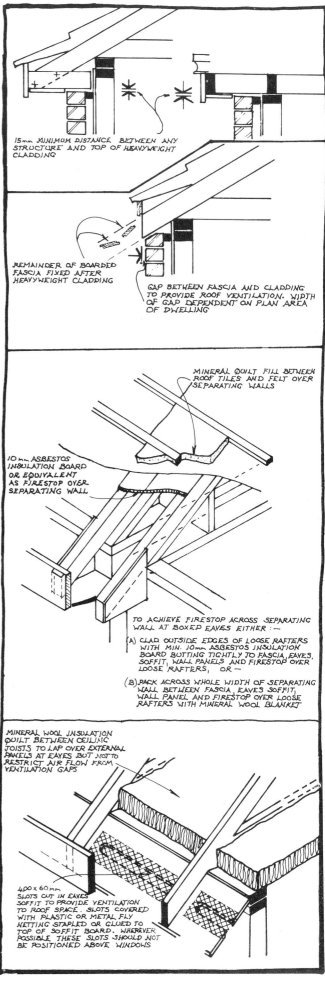

15mm MINIMUM DISTANCE BETWEEN ANY STRUCTURE AND TOP OF HEAVYWEIGHT CLADDING

REMAINDER OF BOARDED FASCIA FIXED AFTER HEAVYWEIGHT CLADDING

GAP BETWEEN FASCIA AND CLADDING TO PROVIDE ROOF VENTILATION. WIDTH OF GAP DEPENDENT ON PLAN AREA OF DWELLING

MINERAL QUILT FILL BETWEEN ROOF TILES AND FELT OVER SEPARATING WALLS

10 mm ASBESTOS INSULATION BOARD OR EQUIVALENT AS FIRESTOP OVER SEPARATING WALL

TO ACHIEVE FIRESTOP ACROSS SEPARATING WALL AT BOXED EAVES EITHER :—

(A) CLAD OUTSIDE EDGES OF LOOSE RAFTERS WITH MIN. 10mm ASBESTOS INSULATION BOARD BUTTING TIGHTLY TO FASCIA, EAVES, SOFFIT, WALL PANELS AND FIRESTOP OVER LOOSE RAFTERS, OR —

(B) PACK ACROSS WHOLE WIDTH OF SEPARATING WALL BETWEEN FASCIA, EAVES SOFFIT, WALL PANEL AND FIRESTOP OVER LOOSE RAFTERS WITH MINERAL WOOL BLANKET

MINERAL WOOL INSULATION QUILT BETWEEN CEILING JOISTS TO LAP OVER EXTERNAL PANELS AT EAVES BUT NOT TO RESTRICT AIR FLOW FROM VENTILATION GAPS

400 x 60 mm SLOTS CUT IN EAVES SOFFIT TO PROVIDE VENTILATION TO ROOF SPACE. SLOTS COVERED WITH PLASTIC OR METAL FLY NETTING STAPLED OR GLUED TO TOP OF SOFFIT BOARD. WHEREVER POSSIBLE THESE SLOTS SHOULD NOT BE POSITIONED ABOVE WINDOWS

Finishing off Inside

General

Finishing off inside can start as soon as all wiring and pipework in wall frames and ceilings have been completed. Before the work proceeds, all extra studs and noggings needed to carry plasterboard linings are fixed. So are all pieces needed to carry lightweight partitions, as well as sanitary and other fittings.

Separating walls

Cavity barriers must first be fixed in any separating walls. 50 mm thick wire reinforced mineral quilt is used which, being flexible, does not tend to carry noise across the cavity. The quilt is spiked to both frames.

Horizontal cavity barriers are needed at each ceiling level. Further, if the separating wall is more than 8 metres long, a vertical cavity barrier will be needed. This must be sited so that there is no unbroken cavity more than 8 metres long.

Insulation

General

In this Manual we recommend the use of 100 mm quilt in outside walls and roof spaces. This gives a U value of less than 0.40 for both. Also, this same quilt should be used in timber ground floors.

Separating walls

To reduce the spread of noise, a 25 mm quilt is fixed to one of the two frames forming separating walls. This is fixed neatly between the studs.

Outside walls

100 mm quilt is used to insulate outside walls. Rolls 600 mm wide are available. This can be simply wedged between and stapled to studs, immediately before lining out. Lengths should be cut 25 mm oversize so that there is a tight compression fit at the top and bottom.

Roof spaces

100 mm quilt is also used in the ceiling space. This can usually best be done after lining out. Care is needed to ensure that eaves ventilation is not obstructed.

Roof space insulation needs always to be carried over any tanks and pipework. This prevents freezing up in cold weather.

Quilt should be butted against noggings and never humped over them or roof bracing as open pockets of cold air might result.

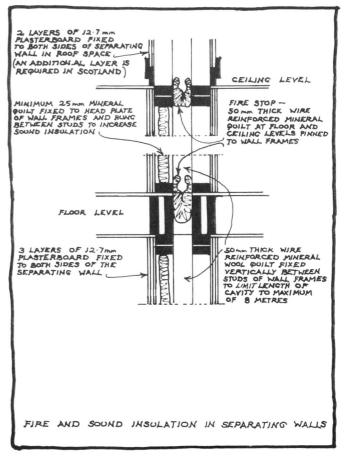

FIRE AND SOUND INSULATION IN SEPARATING WALLS

Bathroom or pipe noise

100 mm quilt may also be used within partitions around bathrooms and wc's or within duct casings to reduce noise to adjacent habitable rooms.

Vapour barrier

A vapour barrier is needed on the inside face of all external wall frames, on the warm side of the insulation.

Polyethylene sheeting or aluminium foil backed plasterboard is used in the NBA/TRADA Method.

Polyethylene sheeting is usually fixed in room height bands and stapled to the face of the wall frames. Laps must be at least 100 mm wide and must occur only directly over the framing. At all laps both layers are thus stapled down together.

The sheeting must be carefully dressed into the reveals of any openings in the outside walls up to the window frames.

There is a risk of condensation in the insulation behind any hole or tear in the sheeting, so any such holes must be made good. Where pipes or wires pass through the sheeting, adhesive tape is used to keep the vapour barrier effectively continuous.

Lining out

In the NBA/TRADA Method, 12.7 mm plasterboard is used throughout, in 1200 mm wide sheets. A single layer is used generally on walls and ceilings. Taper-edged board is recommended, joints being sealed with filler, tape and finishing compound. It is fully explained in manufacturers' manuals.

On separating walls, multiple layers of 12.7 mm plasterboard are used. Three layers are applied inside the dwelling and this is reduced to two layers in the roof space except in Scotland.

In order to prevent any small gaps through which noise might penetrate, vertical joints are staggered from one layer to the next. Any rough cut edges and open joints must be carefully filled, before the next layer is fixed.

The first layer is fixed with 40 mm plasterboard nails at 300 mm centres to all backing members. The second layer is fixed through the first with 60 mm plasterboard nails at 150 mm centres to all backing members. The third layer, to the main body of a separating wall, is bonded in accordance with the instructions of the plasterboard manufacturer who will also supply the bonding material. Any extra costs in bonding the final layer should be offset by savings in preparing the face for decoration.

Single layer 12.7 mm plasterboard used to line external and other internal walls is fixed with 40 mm plasterboard nails at 150 mm centres in the usual way.

Lightweight partitions

For all partitions not carrying floor joists or resisting wind forces lightweight partition systems as in other housing can be used. Heavyweight methods, such as brick and concrete block, should not be used.

Timber frame partitions are very satisfactory and are commonly used. They involve the same materials and methods as the rest of the structure and can be used to provide extra resistance to wind forces in very exposed situations.

72 x 44 mm (75 x 47 mm processed) pieces are used to frame up the partitions, with studs at 600 mm centres. Since the framing does not carry loads from the structure, openings are simply framed up. No lintels are needed.

On small contracts such framing is usually best made up on site, although the main framing may be factory-made.

Where the partitions meet other walls, extra studs have to be introduced into them to form satisfactory junctions which provide fixings for all abutting sheets of plasterboard. These will be of the standard structural stud dimensions of 97 x 44 mm and are fixed before the main structure is lined out.

The framing is lined with 12.7 mm plasterboard as applied to the main structure. Before this is fixed 100 mm quilt insulation is placed in partitions where sound reduction is important, usually compressed to 72 mm. This will always include partitions separating habitable rooms from bathrooms and WC's.

Extra steps to limit the risks of condensation

If this Manual is carefully followed, the risks of condensation problems in the finished dwelling will be limited.

Condensation on interior wall surfaces is much less likely with timber frame construction than with heavy construction, especially with intermittent heating.

Condensation within the external wall construction is well guarded against by using:
(a) vapour checks immediately behind the internal linings;
(b) claddings which are able to "breathe" to the outside;
(c) timber frameworks which are preservative treated.

The remaining concern is with condensation on window panes. In normal housing of masonry construction risks of condensation on outside walls and windows are increased where occupiers are trying to save on heating costs. Main rooms may go unheated for long periods, leading to cold surfaces. Paraffin heaters may be used; these fill the dwelling with water vapour. It is very much with these risks in mind that we recommend high standards of insulation in this Manual. 100 mm quilt is used throughout for outside walls and roof spaces. As a result, heating costs are normally about a third less than in dwellings built to current minimum standards. So the risk of condensation caused by inadequate or unsuitable heating is reduced.

Some occupiers tend in other ways to fill their dwellings with water vapour. This may be from cooking, laundering, or frequent baths. To reduce such problems, extract fans should be installed in kitchens, bathrooms and any separate utility rooms.

Such fans need to be at high level, and as near as possible to the source of steam. It is often better to fit them directly into outer walls, rather than into windows.

Specialist advice may be needed where there are heating boilers in kitchens or utility rooms. The fan must never be able to set up a down-draught in any flue. So a correctly sized and sited fresh-air inlet will be needed.

In other main rooms, it will help if it is possible to have slight ventilation in cold weather. Small opening lights are useful or window frames with separate built-in adjustable or permanent vents.

Despite all these steps, condensation may form on the inside of windows from time to time. Double glazing will reduce but not eliminate the risk. This is greatest at night, when the heating is turned down, especially behind closed curtains. If possible, use windows designed so that any condensation collecting on transoms and sills is drained away outside.

Finishing off Outside

In this chapter we describe how the outside of a timber frame dwelling can be completed. This Manual offers a choice of claddings which may be used. Other claddings have been successfully used on timber frame houses. These include, amongst others:

(a) slates or synthetic slates hung vertically;

(b) rendering applied to metal lathing or proprietary lathing fixed over the sheathing plywood;

(c) vertical timber boarding, of various types, including board on board or board and batten;

(d) GRP with integral aggregate face, fixed with a small airspace between it and the plywood sheathing.

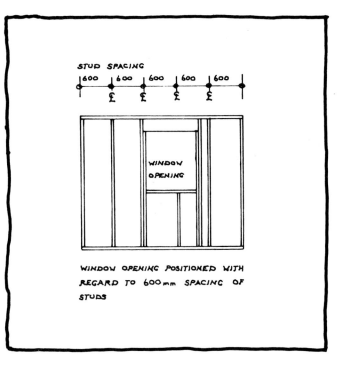

The use of any of these will not affect the structural design as set out in this Manual. However, specialist advice from TRADA and/or manufacturers of claddings should be obtained.

As in other chapters, we deal here only with matters which are special to timber frame construction. So we make only brief reference to materials and techniques also found in other types of housebuilding, such as brickwork or tile hanging.

The rest of this section is set out as follows:

(1) Windows and external doors.

(2) Cavity barriers.

(3) Breather paper.

(4) Lightweight cladding: shiplap boarding, tiles and slates.

(5) Heavyweight cladding: brickwork and concrete blockwork.

(6) Both types of cladding used together.

1 Windows and external doors

Dimensions

If possible, frames which are supplied in multiples of 300 mm widths should be used. They should be so placed in the dwelling that at least one edge is against a stud set at the regular 600 mm spacing. As we explain in the Introduction, this can save on the number of studs needed. It also keeps useless offcuts of sheathing and plasterboard to a minimum.

WINDOW OPENING POSITIONED WITH REGARD TO 600 mm SPACING OF STUDS

Door frames should be 2.100 mm high. Other main openings should be set out so that the heads are also 2.100 mm above floor level. This suits the lintels used in the Method. It also suits any brick coursing.

Materials

Timber windows provide for easy fixing and reduce the risks of condensation on the frames. If metal windows are used they should be set in preservative treated softwood sub frames to achieve a watertight fit to the structural opening. Provision should be made to drain away any condensation forming at the bottom of the metal frame.

Fixing of windows

The precise details of fixing will vary, depending on the cladding.

Any cavity between the timber structure and the cladding must be closed at every opening.

Precisely how this is done will vary with the type of cladding. But the cavities are always closed with a 38 mm thickness of preservative treated softwood. This is fixed to the sheathing before the frames are erected.

With heavyweight cladding, the opening should be framed up all round using a 50 × 38 mm batten.

With lightweight cladding, as shown in this Manual, generally a 38 × 19 mm batten is used to frame up openings. This will need to be varied at the head where vertical tiling is used. A fillet piece will be required to carry the first row of tiles over the window.

Flashings around windows

The joint between the frames and the structure must be made completely weathertight. Dpc's are used at heads, jambs and sills for this purpose. Generally a black polyethylene dpc is used. In most cases a width of 225 mm is suitable. With lightweight cladding, a lead or other suitable metal flashing is used at the sill. This is dressed over the top of the cladding.

Dpc's to jambs and sills are always fixed to frames before they are erected. They are fixed into the rebate on the back face of jambs, and on the underside of sills, using clout nails at 150 mm centres.

Note that dpc's to heads are fixed to the sheathing at the same time as the breather paper.

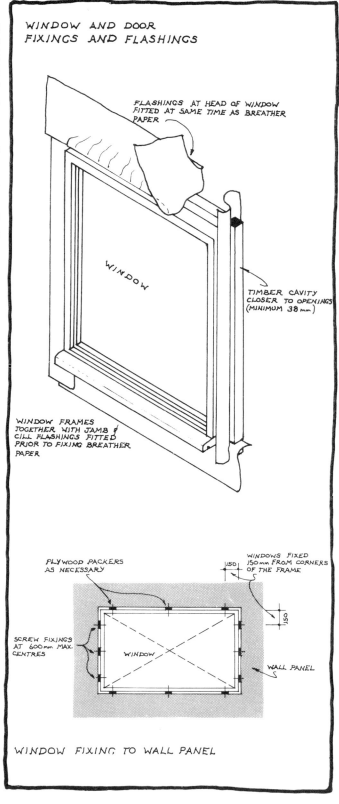

Fixing of window frames

After dpc's have been fixed to jambs and sills, and the opening framed up with cavity barriers, the frames are offered up. Plywood packers are used as necessary between frame and wall panels. The frame is then screwed into position at not less than 600 mm centres.

The first screw in any member is kept 150 mm away from the end of the frame. At least 8 screws should be used all round on small frames, fixing the frames in position according to the type of cladding selected (see later in this chapter).

2 Cavity barriers

The need for all openings to be framed up with cavity barriers has already been described. Depending on the type of cladding, further cavity barriers will be needed. They are required to limit the possible spread of fire. These barriers are also carried out using 38 mm thick softwood battens which have been preservative treated.

With heavyweight cladding, the 50 mm cavity must be closed at the top under the roof eaves and verges. The cavity must be closed vertically at each external corner, and at separating walls. Two barriers are used at separating walls, one for each leaf. Further vertical barriers will be needed in outside walls more than 8 metres long. Such extra barriers must be placed so that there is no unbroken cavity more than 8 metres long.

50 × 38 mm preservative treated battens are used, with black polyethylene dpc's to keep the battens from being in direct contact with the brickwork or blockwork. With vertical barriers, a 50 mm wide polyethylene dpc is face fixed; with horizontal barriers, a 225 mm dpc is used and breather paper must lap a minimum of 75 mm over the top edge. But note that under eaves and verges there will be weather protection, so a face-fixed dpc is used in these positions.

Lightweight claddings shown in this Manual are carried on 38 × 19 mm preservative treated battens.

Where vertical battens are used for horizontal boarding, no vertical cavity barriers will be needed. But horizontal barriers will be required at the top of walling under verges.

Where horizontal battens are used, for instance to carry tile hanging, no horizontal barriers will be needed. But vertical barriers will be required at external corners and at separating walls. Two barriers are used at separating walls, one for each leaf. Further barriers will be needed in any run of horizontal battens more than 8 metres long. Such extra barriers must be placed so that there is no unbroken cavity more than 8 metres long. In both cases, 38 × 19 mm preservative treated battens are used.

Where light and heavyweight claddings are used together, the edge of the cavity behind the heavyweight cladding must be closed off with a 50 × 38 mm batten, a 38 × 19 mm batten is butted against this on the side of the lightweight cladding. Both battens which are preservative treated are protected by a black polyethylene dpc dressed over their outer faces and fixed to the timber structure.

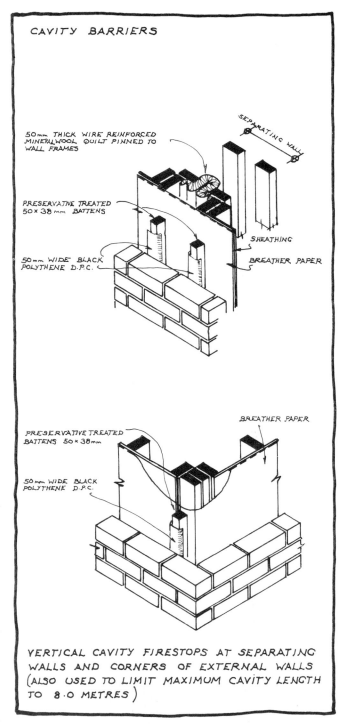

CAVITY BARRIERS

50 mm THICK WIRE REINFORCED MINERALWOOL QUILT PINNED TO WALL FRAMES

SEPARATING WALL

PRESERVATIVE TREATED 50 x 38 mm BATTENS

SHEATHING

BREATHER PAPER

50 mm WIDE BLACK POLYTHENE D.P.C.

BREATHER PAPER

PRESERVATIVE TREATED BATTENS 50 x 38 mm

50 mm WIDE BLACK POLYTHENE D.P.C.

VERTICAL CAVITY FIRESTOPS AT SEPARATING WALLS AND CORNERS OF EXTERNAL WALLS (ALSO USED TO LIMIT MAXIMUM CAVITY LENGTH TO 8.0 METRES)

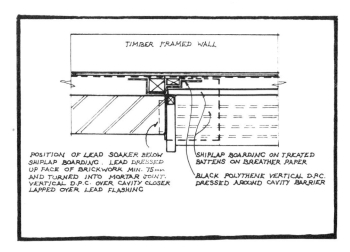

TIMBER FRAMED WALL

POSITION OF LEAD SOAKER BELOW SHIPLAP BOARDING. LEAD DRESSED UP FACE OF BRICKWORK MIN. 75mm AND TURNED INTO MORTAR JOINT. VERTICAL D.P.C. OVER CAVITY CLOSER LAPPED OVER LEAD FLASHING

SHIPLAP BOARDING ON TREATED BATTENS ON BREATHER PAPER

BLACK POLYTHENE VERTICAL D.P.C. DRESSED AROUND CAVITY BARRIER

3 Breather paper

After external joinery is fixed, but before the exterior of the dwelling is clad, the timber frame is faced with breather paper.

As explained in the introduction, this protects the timber structure from any rainwater that may get behind the cladding. It is a special type of building paper, being waterproof but not impervious to water vapour. So the timber frame can dry out after occupation, but condensation will not form on its inside face. For details of what to specify or order, see Chapter 2.3.

Another reason for using the breather paper is to reduce air infiltration through joints between and around panels. It should be lapped and fixed to do this effectively.

Breather paper is fixed to the outside face of the sheathing in horizontal bands, starting from the foundations and working upwards. The first band is fixed so that the bottom edge is 50 mm below the dpc. This ensures that base plates are well protected.

At horizontal joints laps must be at least 100 mm. At vertical joints laps must be at least 150 mm. The breather paper is nailed or stapled to the studs and to the top and bottom timbers of the walling at 150 mm centres.

Breather paper can get torn in high winds, so it is best to fix it just before cladding starts.

The breather paper must be lapped over all dpc's at the heads and jambs of openings. It is fixed directly to the sheathing under the dpc or flashing to each sill.

Except those at openings, all vertical cavity barriers are fixed after the breather paper. So are horizontal barriers directly under eaves and verges. Vertical battens carrying any lightweight cladding are also fixed after the breather paper.

4 Lightweight cladding

Two types of lightweight cladding are recommended, horizontal shiplap boarding and vertical tiles.

Shiplap boarding must have a finished thickness of at least 16 mm. Softwood must be preservative treated. A water repellent stain finish is recommended. This allows the timber to dry out in fine weather. Gloss paint should not be used unless high standards of initial application and maintenance can be relied on. Repainting will always be needed as soon as the paint film starts to fail. *Varnish should not be used.*

External corners and window jambs are finished with a vertical batten of the same thickness as the boarding. At sills, the metal flashing already fixed to the frames is

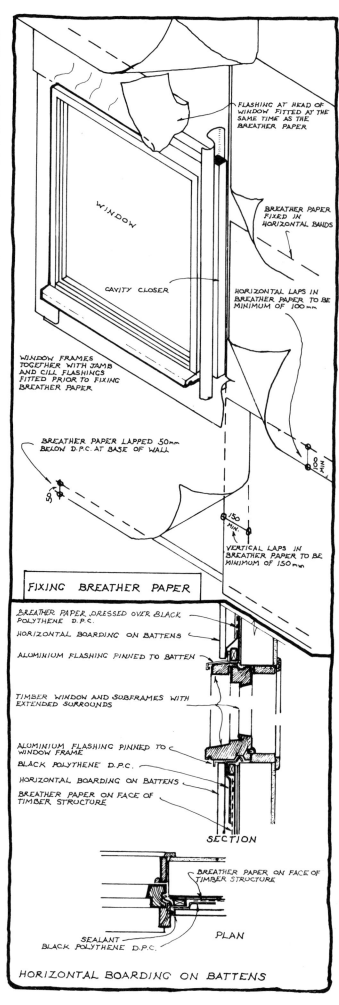

FLASHING AT HEAD OF WINDOW FITTED AT THE SAME TIME AS THE BREATHER PAPER

BREATHER PAPER FIXED IN HORIZONTAL BANDS

WINDOW

CAVITY CLOSER

HORIZONTAL LAPS IN BREATHER PAPER TO BE MINIMUM OF 100 mm

WINDOW FRAMES TOGETHER WITH JAMB AND CILL FLASHINGS FITTED PRIOR TO FIXING BREATHER PAPER

BREATHER PAPER LAPPED 50 mm BELOW D.P.C. AT BASE OF WALL

50

150 MIN.

100 MIN

VERTICAL LAPS IN BREATHER PAPER TO BE MINIMUM OF 150 mm

FIXING BREATHER PAPER

BREATHER PAPER DRESSED OVER BLACK POLYTHENE D.P.C.
HORIZONTAL BOARDING ON BATTENS
ALUMINIUM FLASHING PINNED TO BATTEN

TIMBER WINDOW AND SUBFRAMES WITH EXTENDED SURROUNDS

ALUMINIUM FLASHING PINNED TO WINDOW FRAME
BLACK POLYTHENE D.P.C.
HORIZONTAL BOARDING ON BATTENS
BREATHER PAPER ON FACE OF TIMBER STRUCTURE

SECTION

BREATHER PAPER ON FACE OF TIMBER STRUCTURE

SEALANT
BLACK POLYTHENE D.P.C.

PLAN

HORIZONTAL BOARDING ON BATTENS

dressed down over the top board. If boarding is used across the ends of separating walls, a fire stop is required at this position within the cavity immediately behind the boarding. Mineral quilt is used, compressed into the space.

Vertical tile hanging can be carried out as in other housing. A tilting fillet will be needed to carry the bottom row. This will include the bottom row over openings. These fillets must be protected by a dpc lapped under the breather paper.

At sills the lead or other metal flashing, already fixed to the frame, is dressed over the top row of tiles.

The spaces behind the tiling will need to be fire stopped at separating walls and at vertical cavity barriers. This can be done by carefully bedding the tiles down on mineral wool compressed between the tiling battens. At the jambs of openings of windows without extended head and jamb sections mortar is pointed up between the tiles to form a neat finish and close the cavities.

5 Heavyweight cladding

Brickwork or concrete blockwork cladding may be used, fair faced or rendered. This is carried out as a single leaf, with a 50 mm cavity behind. As explained in the introduction, such heavyweight cladding is built directly off the foundations. Its weight is not carried by the timber structure, so at openings there must be lintels to carry the cladding. These are quite separate from those in the timber frame construction. Galvanised mild steel angles may be suitable. Proprietary lintels specially designed for

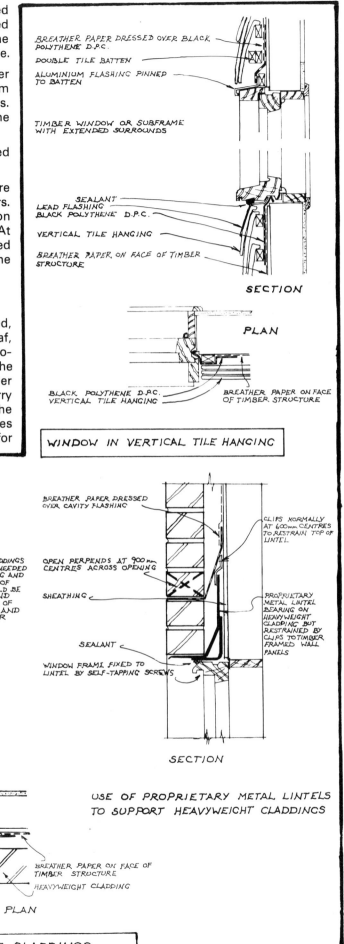

BREATHER PAPER DRESSED OVER BLACK POLYTHENE D.P.C.
DOUBLE TILE BATTEN
ALUMINIUM FLASHING PINNED TO BATTEN

TIMBER WINDOW OR SUBFRAME WITH EXTENDED SURROUNDS

SEALANT
LEAD FLASHING
BLACK POLYTHENE D.P.C.
VERTICAL TILE HANGING
BREATHER PAPER ON FACE OF TIMBER STRUCTURE

SECTION

PLAN

BLACK POLYTHENE D.P.C.
VERTICAL TILE HANGING

BREATHER PAPER ON FACE OF TIMBER STRUCTURE

WINDOW IN VERTICAL TILE HANGING

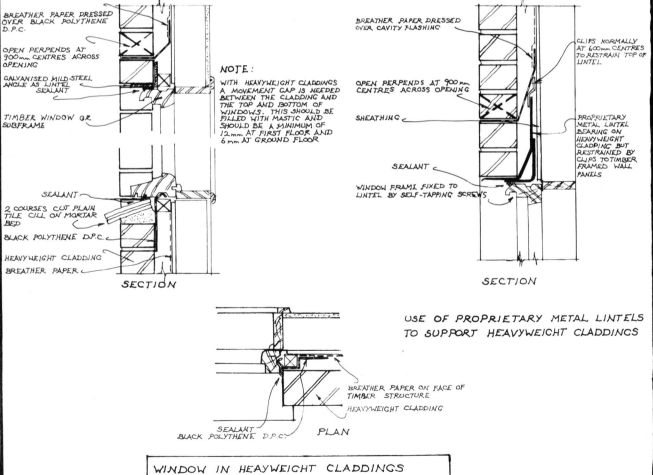

BREATHER PAPER DRESSED OVER BLACK POLYTHENE D.P.C.
OPEN PERPENDS AT 900 mm CENTRES ACROSS OPENING
GALVANISED MILD STEEL ANGLE AS LINTEL
SEALANT
TIMBER WINDOW OR SUBFRAME

NOTE:
WITH HEAVYWEIGHT CLADDINGS A MOVEMENT GAP IS NEEDED BETWEEN THE CLADDING AND THE TOP AND BOTTOM OF WINDOWS. THIS SHOULD BE FILLED WITH MASTIC AND SHOULD BE A MINIMUM OF 12 mm AT FIRST FLOOR AND 6 mm AT GROUND FLOOR

SEALANT
2 COURSES CUT PLAIN TILE CILL ON MORTAR BED
BLACK POLYTHENE D.P.C.
HEAVYWEIGHT CLADDING
BREATHER PAPER

SECTION

BREATHER PAPER DRESSED OVER CAVITY FLASHING

OPEN PERPENDS AT 900 mm CENTRES ACROSS OPENING

SHEATHING

SEALANT

WINDOW FRAME FIXED TO LINTEL BY SELF-TAPPING SCREWS

CLIPS NORMALLY AT 600 mm CENTRES TO RESTRAIN TOP OF LINTEL

PROPRIETARY METAL LINTEL BEARING ON HEAVYWEIGHT CLADDING BUT RESTRAINED BY CLIPS TO TIMBER FRAMED WALL PANELS

SECTION

USE OF PROPRIETARY METAL LINTELS TO SUPPORT HEAVYWEIGHT CLADDINGS

BREATHER PAPER ON FACE OF TIMBER STRUCTURE
HEAVYWEIGHT CLADDING

SEALANT
BLACK POLYTHENE D.P.C.

PLAN

WINDOW IN HEAVYWEIGHT CLADDINGS

heavy cladding to timber frame constructions are available.

The brickwork or blockwork must be carried out so as to allow slight vertical shrinkage of the timber structure. For this reason flexible wall ties must be used. These are fixed back through the breather paper and sheathing into the studs at 600 mm centres.

Under most circumstances rows of ties not more than 400 mm apart vertically will be suitable. In brickwork, this will mean every fifth course. As in cavity masonry, more ties may occasionally be needed on exposed sites. This is most likely to occur where there are narrow gaps between the gable-ends of dwellings.

Also, as in normal cavity masonry, the type of tie used needs to be chosen with care to avoid risks of failure through corrosion, especially if the masonry extends beyond first floor level. Metal strip ties of stainless steel or of mild steel with a zinc coating of not less than $260g/m^2$ as specified in BS 1243:1978 will be suitable. Other ties approved by the Agrément Board for timber frame construction will also be suitable. As already explained, to allow for movement, a gap of at least 15 mm must be left at the top of heavyweight cladding under eaves and verges.

For the same reason allowance for 12 mm movement should be made at upper storey window sills and 6 mm at ground storey sills.

Weep holes are needed to drain the cavity at dpc's. These will be needed at the heads of openings and at all horizontal cavity barriers, except those directly under eaves and verges. Ventilation will be needed at the base of the cavity walls. Every fourth perpend in the brick course immediately below the damp proof course should be left open to provide cavity ventilation.

As in normal cavity work, every effort needs to be made on site to prevent the cavity from becoming filled with mortar droppings. The base of the cavity should be filled with mortar to a level approximately 200 mm below ground level.

If concrete blocks or bricks are used, do not forget to provide vertical joints to allow for shrinkage, when widths of masonry exceed 6 metres Similarly movement joints will also be required for calcium silicate (sand lime) bricks when widths exceed 6–7.5 metres. With clay bricks this dimension should not generally exceed 12 metres. Vertical movement joints should be filled with an appropriate material and finished with a sealant as recommended by CP 121: Part 1: 1976 "Walling". It is important that such fillers and sealants permit movement to occur and the joints are not accidentally filled with mortar droppings etc. Do not use too strong a mortar and make sure that the bricks are cured before laying.

6 Both types of cladding used together

Many timber frame dwellings are built in the UK using both types of cladding together. For instance brickwork or blockwork is often limited to vertical panels between the openings. Lightweight cladding is used above and below the windows. This avoids the need for lintels in the heavyweight cladding. Allowance for movement is not needed at sills, but only where the brickwork meets the eaves and verges. Allowance for slip movement between the sides of the window frames and the brickwork is also needed.

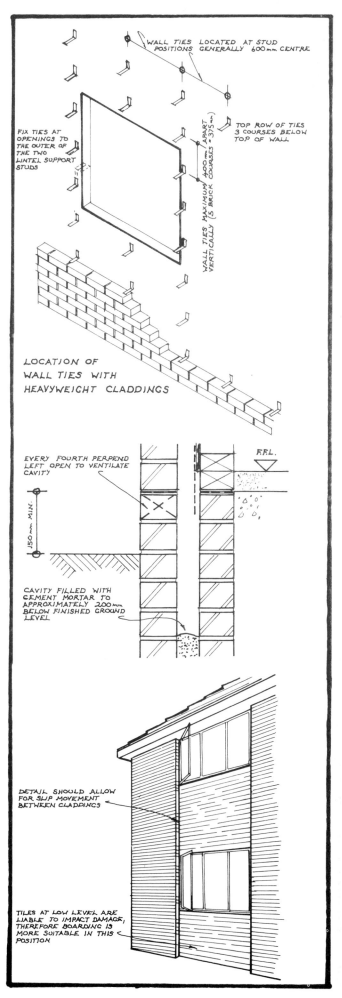

WALL TIES LOCATED AT STUD POSITIONS GENERALLY 600mm CENTRE

FIX TIES AT OPENINGS TO THE OUTER OF THE TWO LINTEL SUPPORT STUDS

TOP ROW OF TIES 3 COURSES BELOW TOP OF WALL

WALL TIES MAXIMUM 400mm APART VERTICALLY (5 BRICK COURSES = 375mm)

LOCATION OF WALL TIES WITH HEAVYWEIGHT CLADDINGS

EVERY FOURTH PERPEND LEFT OPEN TO VENTILATE CAVITY

F.F.L.

150mm MIN.

CAVITY FILLED WITH CEMENT MORTAR TO APPROXIMATELY 200mm BELOW FINISHED GROUND LEVEL

DETAIL SHOULD ALLOW FOR SLIP MOVEMENT BETWEEN CLADDINGS

TILES AT LOW LEVEL ARE LIABLE TO IMPACT DAMAGE, THEREFORE BOARDING IS MORE SUITABLE IN THIS POSITION

Vertical joints between light and heavy cladding need to be made weathertight. A vertical cavity barrier 50 mm by 38 mm is needed, as already described, behind the edge of the brickwork or blockwork. A vertical batten for the lightweight cladding is butted against it. A black polyethylene dpc is then dressed over both. With shiplap boarding the joint will need to be finished with a cover piece.

Another method often used is to limit brickwork or blockwork to the ground floor of two storey dwellings. This is often done in local authority housing. The use of bricks or blocks is thus limited to those areas likely to suffer damage from impact or vandals. The top of the heavyweight cladding is usually lined up with the window heads on the ground floor.

The simplest way of protecting the top of the heavyweight cladding is to flare out the lightweight cladding above it with sprocket pieces. With vertically hung tiles the treatment can be carried round to the flank walls with carefully fixed corner tiles. A small amount of cutting of abutting tiles may be needed in the lower courses.

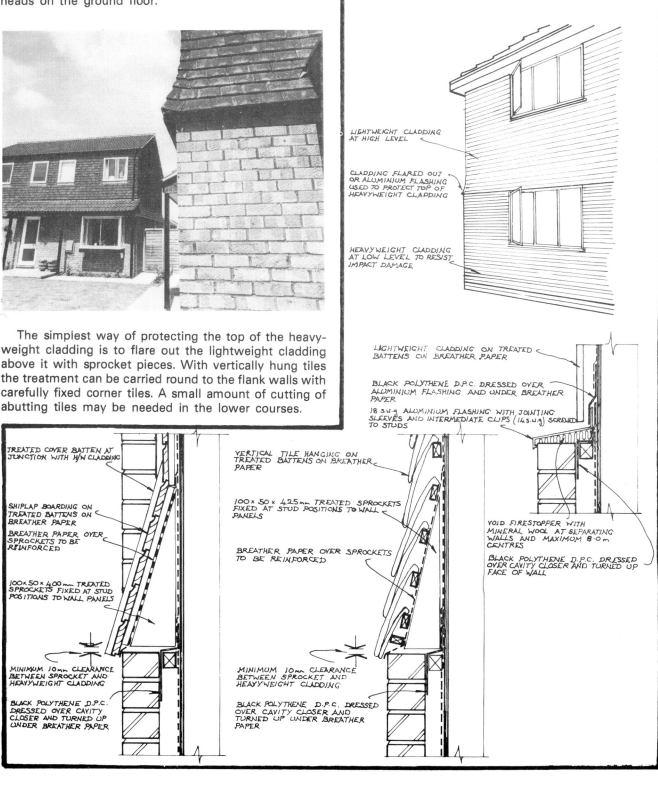

TIMBER FRAMED WALL

POSITION OF LEAD SOAKER BELOW SHIPLAP BOARDING. LEAD DRESSED UP FACE OF BRICKWORK MIN. 75mm AND TURNED INTO MORTAR JOINT. VERTICAL D.P.C. OVER CAVITY CLOSER LAPPED OVER LEAD FLASHING

SHIPLAP BOARDING ON TREATED BATTENS ON BREATHER PAPER

BLACK POLYTHENE VERTICAL D.P.C. DRESSED AROUND CAVITY BARRIER

LIGHTWEIGHT CLADDING AT HIGH LEVEL

CLADDING FLARED OUT OR ALUMINIUM FLASHING USED TO PROTECT TOP OF HEAVYWEIGHT CLADDING

HEAVYWEIGHT CLADDING AT LOW LEVEL TO RESIST IMPACT DAMAGE

LIGHTWEIGHT CLADDING ON TREATED BATTENS ON BREATHER PAPER

BLACK POLYTHENE D.P.C. DRESSED OVER ALUMINIUM FLASHING AND UNDER BREATHER PAPER

18 S.W.G ALUMINIUM FLASHING WITH JOINTING SLEEVES AND INTERMEDIATE CLIPS (14 S.W.G) SCREWED TO STUDS

VOID FIRESTOPPER WITH MINERAL WOOL AT SEPARATING WALLS AND MAXIMUM 8.0m CENTRES

BLACK POLYTHENE D.P.C. DRESSED OVER CAVITY CLOSER AND TURNED UP FACE OF WALL

TREATED COVER BATTEN AT JUNCTION WITH H/W CLADDING

SHIPLAP BOARDING ON TREATED BATTENS ON BREATHER PAPER

BREATHER PAPER OVER SPROCKETS TO BE REINFORCED

100 x 50 x 400 mm TREATED SPROCKETS FIXED AT STUD POSITIONS TO WALL PANELS

MINIMUM 10mm CLEARANCE BETWEEN SPROCKET AND HEAVYWEIGHT CLADDING

BLACK POLYTHENE D.P.C. DRESSED OVER CAVITY CLOSER AND TURNED UP UNDER BREATHER PAPER

VERTICAL TILE HANGING ON TREATED BATTENS ON BREATHER PAPER

100 x 50 x 425 mm TREATED SPROCKETS FIXED AT STUD POSITIONS TO WALL PANELS

BREATHER PAPER OVER SPROCKETS TO BE REINFORCED

MINIMUM 10mm CLEARANCE BETWEEN SPROCKET AND HEAVYWEIGHT CLADDING

BLACK POLYTHENE D.P.C. DRESSED OVER CAVITY CLOSER AND TURNED UP UNDER BREATHER PAPER

Horizontal timber boarding is less likely to be permitted by regulations on flank walls because of boundary distances. It counts as a 50% unprotected area. It will be more usual to have full height brickwork on the flank wall with returns for a short distance on the front and back walls against which the timber boarding can be butted. If timber boarding is permitted and desired on the side walls, it is possible to carry it around the corner, using a lead soaker behind the flared part and exercising some skill in cutting the boards at the corner. Alternatively, brick corner piers can be used to provide simpler butting details on both sides.

Where the flared out lightweight cladding passes over a window opening, the bottom of the cavity is closed by a preservative treated soffit board, fixed to the bottoms of the sprockets. This should be of 38 mm thick timber or 10 mm asbestos insulation board tightly fitted to act as a fire barrier in case fire breaks through the window opening.

If it is preferred not to use the flared out detail a form of coping and flashing made of 18 SWG aluminium lends itself to detailing which allows for the vertical movement between the top of the masonry and the timber frame.

Details for Steps and Staggers between Attached Houses

Masonry core walls

The following details are based on the use of a concrete blockwork or brickwork core wall built in a widened cavity between standard timber separating wall frames. The masonry leaf is tied to both timber frame leaves with flexible ties. To avoid structural sound transmission, the ties should not be opposite each other.

To reduce airborne sound it must be ensured that the vertical joints between bricks or blocks are effectively pointed or that a rough render is put on one side of the wall.

The expense and awkwardness of building the core wall between the timber frames will be partly offset by reducing the plasterboard linings to two layers instead of three in rooms and one layer instead of two in attics. The mineral wool normally required on one side of the cavity in a separating wall to improve sound insulation is not required in this case.

This use of the core wall also simplifies junction details. The core wall can be extended forwards and backwards as the brick external wall cladding; upwards as the stepped gable cladding, and downwards to form part of a retaining wall at steps in ground levels. The various conditions are shown in the diagrams.

It must be remembered that the separating wall zone has to be increased to allow for the thickness of the core wall and so that it can line through with the brick cladding with a 50 mm cavity behind.

Shaded areas show where separating walls become external. The diagrams are based on $22\frac{1}{2}°$ roof pitches but the same principles apply with other pitches.

Stagger only

Increments of 600 mm are preferred although with solid core the dimension is not critical as studs may be tied to the wall at any position.

Step only

The detail at eaves on 'step only' elevations, if heavyweight cladding is not used to first floor elevations, may be solved by building the solid core wall out to the line of fascia.

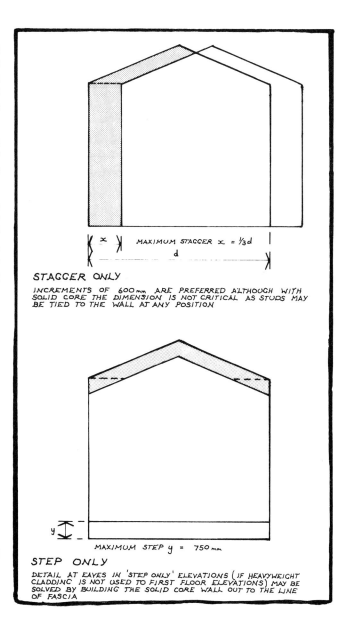

MAXIMUM STAGGER $x = \frac{1}{3}d$

STAGGER ONLY

INCREMENTS OF 600mm ARE PREFERRED ALTHOUGH WITH SOLID CORE THE DIMENSION IS NOT CRITICAL AS STUDS MAY BE TIED TO THE WALL AT ANY POSITION

MAXIMUM STEP y = 750mm

STEP ONLY

DETAIL AT EAVES IN 'STEP ONLY' ELEVATIONS (IF HEAVYWEIGHT CLADDING IS NOT USED TO FIRST FLOOR ELEVATIONS) MAY BE SOLVED BY BUILDING THE SOLID CORE WALL OUT TO THE LINE OF FASCIA

Step + stagger

The diagram shows 600 mm step and 600 mm stagger. The combination of a 300 mm step and 600 mm stagger will result in minimal clearance of verges on one roof slope when the roof pitch is 22½°.

Step + stagger to provide common roof plane on one slope

When there is a step and a stagger, the dimension of the step divided by the dimension of the stagger equals the tangent of the angle of slope. To provide a common roof plane on one slope this angle must be equal to the roof pitch. The diagram shows various related steps and staggers which will provide a common roof plane for a 22½° roof pitch.

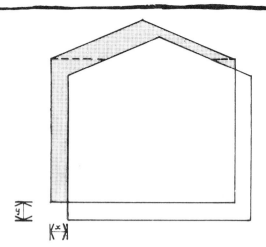

STEP + STAGGER

THE DIAGRAM SHOWS 600 mm STEP AND 600 mm STAGGER. THE COMBINATION OF A 300 mm STEP AND 600 mm STAGGER WILL RESULT IN MINIMAL CLEARANCE OF VERGES ON ONE ROOF SLOPE

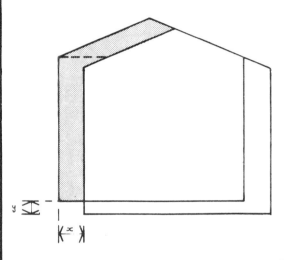

STEP + STAGGER TO PROVIDE COMMON ROOF PLANE ON ONE SLOPE (ROOF PITCH 22½°)

$$\frac{y}{x} = \text{TANGENT } 22½°$$

STAGGER (x)	STEP (y) (IN MULTIPLES OF BRICK COURSES)
724 mm	300 mm
905 mm	375 mm
1086 mm	450 mm
1448 mm	600 mm
1810 mm	750 mm

SHAPED AREAS SHOW WHERE SEPARATING WALLS BECOME EXTERNA

THE DIAGRAMS ARE BASED ON 22½° ROOF PITCHES BUT THE SAME PRINCIPLES APPLY WITH OTHER PITCHES

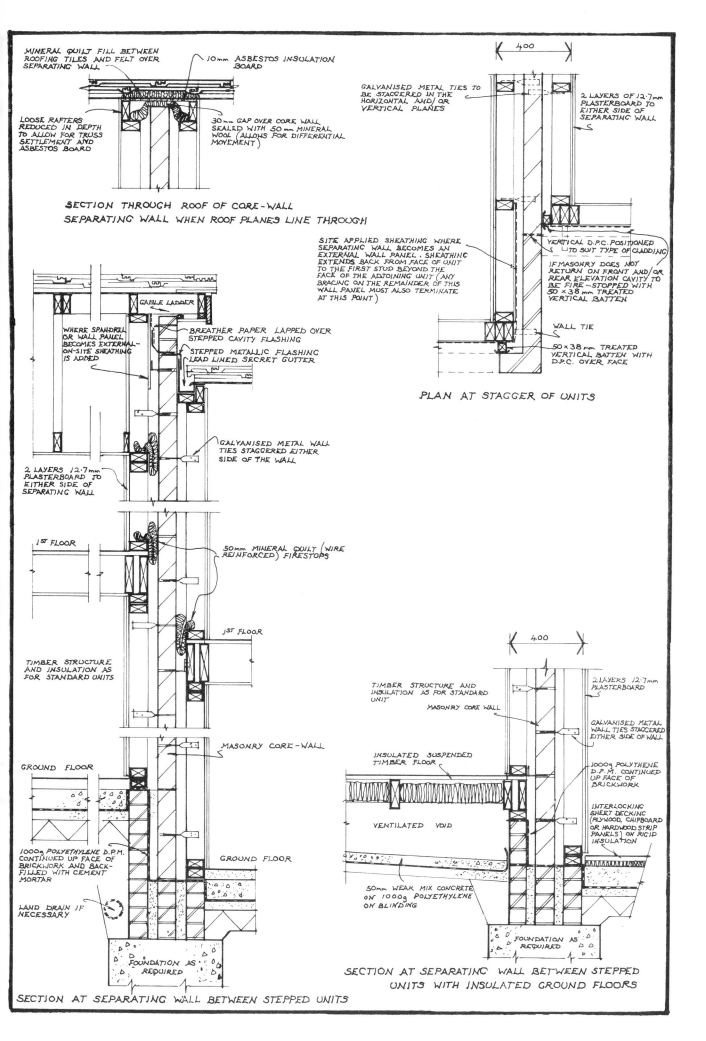

MINERAL QUILT FILL BETWEEN ROOFING TILES AND FELT OVER SEPARATING WALL

10mm ASBESTOS INSULATION BOARD

LOOSE RAFTERS REDUCED IN DEPTH TO ALLOW FOR TRUSS SETTLEMENT AND ASBESTOS BOARD

30 mm GAP OVER CORE WALL SEALED WITH 50 mm MINERAL WOOL (ALLOWS FOR DIFFERENTIAL MOVEMENT)

SECTION THROUGH ROOF OF CORE-WALL SEPARATING WALL WHEN ROOF PLANES LINE THROUGH

GALVANISED METAL TIES TO BE STAGGERED IN THE HORIZONTAL AND/OR VERTICAL PLANES

2 LAYERS OF 12·7mm PLASTERBOARD TO EITHER SIDE OF SEPARATING WALL

VERTICAL D.P.C. POSITIONED TO SUIT TYPE OF CLADDING

IF MASONRY DOES NOT RETURN ON FRONT AND/OR REAR ELEVATION CAVITY TO BE FIRE-STOPPED WITH 50 × 38 mm TREATED VERTICAL BATTEN

WALL TIE

50 × 38 mm TREATED VERTICAL BATTEN WITH D.P.C. OVER FACE

PLAN AT STAGGER OF UNITS

SITE APPLIED SHEATHING WHERE SEPARATING WALL BECOMES AN EXTERNAL WALL PANEL. SHEATHING EXTENDS BACK FROM FACE OF UNIT TO THE FIRST STUD BEYOND THE FACE OF THE ADJOINING UNIT (ANY BRACING ON THE REMAINDER OF THIS WALL PANEL MUST ALSO TERMINATE AT THIS POINT)

GABLE LADDER

WHERE SPANDREL OR WALL PANEL BECOMES EXTERNAL ON-SITE SHEATHING IS ADDED

BREATHER PAPER LAPPED OVER STEPPED CAVITY FLASHING

STEPPED METALLIC FLASHING LEAD LINED SECRET GUTTER

GALVANISED METAL WALL TIES STAGGERED EITHER SIDE OF THE WALL

2 LAYERS 12·7mm PLASTERBOARD TO EITHER SIDE OF SEPARATING WALL

1ST FLOOR

50mm MINERAL QUILT (WIRE REINFORCED) FIRESTOPS

1ST FLOOR

TIMBER STRUCTURE AND INSULATION AS FOR STANDARD UNITS

TIMBER STRUCTURE AND INSULATION AS FOR STANDARD UNIT

MASONRY CORE WALL

INSULATED SUSPENDED TIMBER FLOOR

2 LAYERS 12·7mm PLASTERBOARD

GALVANISED METAL WALL TIES STAGGERED EITHER SIDE OF WALL

GROUND FLOOR

MASONRY CORE-WALL

GROUND FLOOR

VENTILATED VOID

1000g POLYETHYLENE D.P.M. CONTINUED UP FACE OF BRICKWORK

INTERLOCKING SHEET DECKING (PLYWOOD, CHIPBOARD OR HARDWOOD STRIP PANELS) ON RIGID INSULATION

1000g POLYETHYLENE D.P.M. CONTINUED UP FACE OF BRICKWORK AND BACK-FILLED WITH CEMENT MORTAR

LAND DRAIN IF NECESSARY

50mm WEAK MIX CONCRETE ON 1000g POLYETHYLENE ON BLINDING

FOUNDATION AS REQUIRED

FOUNDATION AS REQUIRED

SECTION AT SEPARATING WALL BETWEEN STEPPED UNITS

SECTION AT SEPARATING WALL BETWEEN STEPPED UNITS WITH INSULATED GROUND FLOORS

Designing the Dwelling and its Timber Structure

For simple and effective use of this Manual the dwelling and its timber structure should be designed together. This is done in the following three main stages which are detailed below:

1. *Sketch the design*
2. *Develop the design*
3. *Complete the design*

1 Sketch the design

(i)   Select the appropriate wind category.

To do this locate the site on the wind zone map on page 55 and decide which of zones A, B or C it occurs within. The lines indicating the limits of these zones are the lines of the 44, 48 and 52 m/sec basic wind speeds as defined in British Standard Code of Practice 3: Chapter V: Part 2: 1972. Where any doubt exists as to the appropriate zone reference can be made to this document or to the local building control office.

Next the ground roughness category of the site has to be identified. Three of the ground roughness categories in BSCP 3 are allowed by the NBA/TRADA Method. These are:

Ground roughness category 2. Flat or undulating country with obstructions such as hedges or walls around fields, scattered windbreaks of trees and occasional buildings. Examples are most farmland and country estates with the exception of those parts that are well wooded.

Ground roughness category 3. Surfaces covered by numerous large obstructions. Examples are well-wooded parkland and forest areas, towns and their suburbs, and the outskirts of large cities. The general level of roof-tops and obstructions is assumed at about 10 m, but the category will include built-up areas generally apart from those that qualify for category 4.

Ground roughness category 4. Surfaces covered by numerous large obstructions with a general roof height of about 25 m or more. This category covers only the centres of large towns and cities where the buildings are not only high, but are also not too widely spaced.

Once again, should there be uncertainty as to the

Ground roughness category 2   *Aerofilms Ltd*

Ground roughness category 3   *Aerofilms Ltd*

ground roughness of the site, the local Building Control Officer may well be able to offer advice.

Note that on sites in ground roughness category 1 (long stretches of open, level or near level country with no shelter, such as flat coastal fringes, fens and unfenced countryside), or sites with special features (cliff tops, exposed hillsides etc), specialist advice must be sought.

Taken together, site location and ground roughness category give the wind category, for instance A3 or B2.

(ii) *Decide planning preferences*

*   What sizes of dwellings are required?
*   Is the accommodation to be provided in single or two storey units?
*   What shapes of units and groups of units are most suitable?
*   What roof pitches are to be used?
*   What sizes of openings are appropriate?

Using basic rectangular dwelling types there are many combinations of frontage and depth which provide similar overall areas. The choice of which types are most likely to provide a good layout will depend on many factors but certainly the shape of the site, the position of road access, the density required, and the aspects of the plots will be important matters needing consideration.

Local planning requirements may limit the choice of roof design. Two ranges of roof pitches are permitted within the NBA/TRADA Method 22½°–30°, or 35°–40°. Roof pitches in excess of 30° should not be used for truss spans greater than 8.1 m. The permitted weights of roof covering for each range of roof slopes are given on page 31.

A set of wind charts is included showing the range of dwelling types which may be built in a given location. An example of how the charts are used is given in (iii) below. The following table shows which chart should be used for particular wind zone categories related to numbers of storeys.

Number of storeys	Roof pitch	Wind zone/category	Wind chart number
2 storeys	22½°–30°	A3, A4	1
		A2	2
		B3, B4	3
		B2	4
		C3, C4	5
		C2	6
	35°–40°	A3, A4	7
		A2	8
		B3, B4	9
		B2	10
		C3, C4	11
		C2	12
1 storey	22½°–30°	All	13
	35°–40°	A3, A4	14
		A2, B3, B4	15
		B2, C3, C4	16
		C2	17

The method provides alternative percentage openings for the front and rear elevations of houses, namely 40% and 30%. The former should accommodate all the openings that are required and the latter will normally be perfectly acceptable if high overall thermal insulation

Ground roughness category 3   Aerofilms Lt

Ground roughness category 4   Aerofilms L

is being sought. Gable walls of houses are general assumed to have openings not exceeding 20% of wa areas. In the case of detached houses in the shaded are of the wind charts at the end of this chapter, opening in the 'gable' walls may be increased to 30% if 3 m ru of sheathing is added to an internal wind bracing pane parallel to the gable walls and within the middle third the plan (see page 51). If the relevant chart shows th need for wind bracing in the normal case (see chapte 2.1.2 (ii)) the extra sheathing may be added on the othe side of the wind bracing partition. Alternatively, a furthe length of partitioning may be sheathed (on one side). If higher percentage of openings is required advice shou be sought from the TRADA regional officer. For bunga lows 30% openings are permitted in all external wall

From all these considerations will emerge a group dwelling types and tentative layouts that appear feasible

(iii) *Use wind charts to obtain permissible shell sizes*

With both the wind category and the series of dwelling options preferred now identified, the wind charts can be used to check which of the dwelling options are permissible within the appropriate wind category. Let us suppose that the site is in the suburbs of Nottingham, that the preference is for units of around 90 m² area with 40% openings in main elevations, and a roof pitch of 25°.

The appropriate wind category will be B3. The first assessment of the site has suggested that 5.4 × 8.1 narrow frontage houses will suit some parts of the site, 8.1 × 5.4 wide frontage houses will suit other parts and a group of 12.6 × 7.2 wide frontage bungalows yet another. The appropriate wind charts are 3 and 13.

Looking first at the two storey houses on wind chart 3 we can see that:

> 5.4 frontage × 8.1 deep houses can be built as semi detached, with sheathed internal partitions, or in terraces of three units without. They cannot be built detached.

> 8.1 frontage × 5.4 deep houses can be built in all groupings without the need for sheathed internal partitions.

> 6.6 frontage × 6.6 deep houses, which provide a similar area, can be built in all groupings but detached dwellings will require sheathed internal partitions.

> 8.1 frontage × 5.4 deep detached houses can be built with 30% openings in the gable walls if a 3 m length of sheathed internal partitions is provided parallel to the depth. All other house types can have a maximum of 20% openings in gable walls.

Similarly looking at the single storey wind chart 13 we can see that a 12.6 frontage × 7.2 depth bungalow can be built without sheathed internal partitions.

The charts for single storey dwellings (bungalows) have been prepared on the following assumptions:

(a) Dual pitched roofs only are permitted with maximum span 10.2 m for roof pitches in the range $22\frac{1}{2}°–30°$ and 8.1 m for roof pitches in the range 35°–40°. All roofs will be formed to span the shorter distance between external walls.

(b) The terms frontage and depth have no significance in terms of siting.

(c) When 'L'-shaped plans are used the junction of the roofs at the return must be constructed in the manner shown. 'L'-shaped plans should not be used for roof pitches in the range 35°–40°. Ends of trussed rafters should be supported internally on a wall constructed as an external wall panel but without the plywood sheathing. Studs should be nogged at mid height. Openings should be provided with lintels and cripple studs as on page 53. The maximum single opening that can be provided is 2100 mm but two such openings side by side can be used provided that the lintel members are continuous over a central post formed from 4 standard studs bolted together. The top of any central post is to be fixed to the continuous lintel member with two galvanised steel nail plates each with at least 4 nails into the top of the post and 4 into the lintel. At the bottom it should be supported by an independent foundation or a thickened concrete

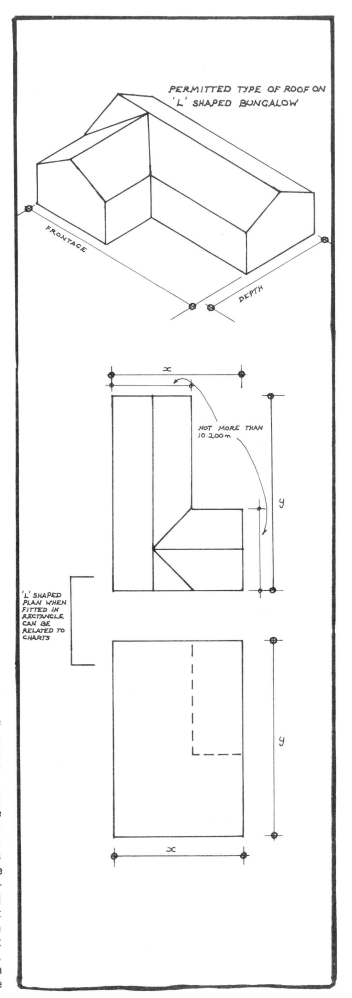

PERMITTED TYPE OF ROOF ON 'L' SHAPED BUNGALOW

FRONTAGE

DEPTH

NOT MORE THAN 10.200 m

'L' SHAPED PLAN WHEN FITTED IN RECTANGLE CAN BE RELATED TO CHARTS slab. The post should be fixed with two galvanised steel straps, each with 4 nails into the timber. The other ends are to be cast or grouted into the concrete slab/foundation. A concrete slab or pad without reinforcement should be at least 350 mm thick within 400 mm of the centre of the post.

(d) 'L'-shaped plans may be formed *within* any rectangular shape indicated on the charts provided that conditions (a) to (c) above are complied with.

(e) The total area of openings in any external wall must not exceed 30% of the area of the wall. Return walls in 'L' shaped plans must be considered individually.

(iv) *Prepare alternative site layouts*

Trial layouts can now be prepared using the dwelling types selected in (ii) above. If second thoughts occur on whether another dwelling type may be preferable in a certain part of the site reference can be made back to the wind charts to see if this is possible.

2 Develop the design

(i) *Select a preferred site layout from the preliminary arrangements*

(ii) *Complete internal layouts in sketch form*

With the exception of 'L'-shaped bungalows referred to in 1(iii) above, only simple rectangular floor plans may be used. Studs, floor joists and trussed rafters must always be at 600 mm spacings. Best use of the structure will therefore be made if its width and depth are both multiples of 600 mm.

These dimensions are measured to the inside face of the framing.

If this is not possible the most economical use of the trussed rafters will be achieved if at least the width of the dwelling is a multiple of 600 mm. Failing this, use 300 mm multiples. Note that all roofs are assumed in the method to be dual pitched and to have a maximum span of 10.2 metres. (8.1 m in the case of roof pitches in excess of 30°).

With two storey dwellings it is necessary to avoid any overhangs or set-backs at first floor level. In two storey

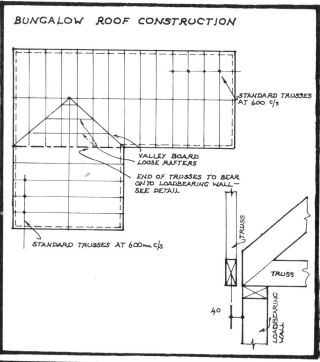

BUNGALOW ROOF CONSTRUCTION

STANDARD TRUSSES AT 600 c/s
VALLEY BOARD LOOSE RAFTERS
END OF TRUSSES TO BEAR ON TO LOADBEARING WALL — SEE DETAIL
STANDARD TRUSSES AT 600mm c/s
TRUSS
TRUSS
40
LOADBEARING WALL

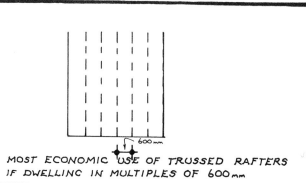

600 mm

MOST ECONOMIC USE OF TRUSSED RAFTERS IF DWELLING IN MULTIPLES OF 600 mm

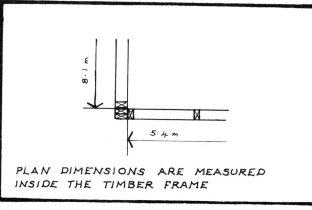

8.1 m
5.4 m

PLAN DIMENSIONS ARE MEASURED INSIDE THE TIMBER FRAME

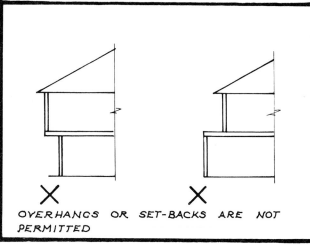

X   X

OVERHANGS OR SET-BACKS ARE NOT PERMITTED

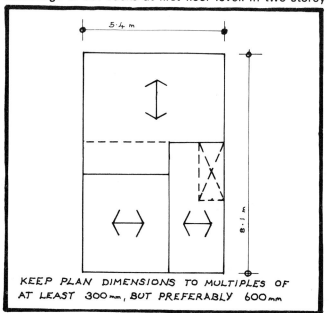

5.4 m

8.1 m

KEEP PLAN DIMENSIONS TO MULTIPLES OF AT LEAST 300 mm, BUT PREFERABLY 600 mm

dwellings it will probably be necessary to carry upper floor joists on one or more loadbearing partitions.

Joists are included in tables on page 53 which can span up to a maximum of 3.9 metres clear between wall frames. Except round stairs, both ends of every joist must be carried on a wall frame.

Particular care must be taken to incorporate any sheathed internal partitions indicated by the wind charts. These may be required parallel to either the gable or the frontage. In some cases they may be required parallel to both the gable and the frontage. The length of panel height internal sheathing to be provided in such cases is as follows:

Sheathed internal partitions parallel to depth	3 m or ½ dwelling depth, whichever is the greater.
Sheathed internal partitions parallel to frontage	3 m or ½ dwelling frontage, whichever is the greater.

Chart symbols indicate as follows:

☐   Sheathed internal partition required parallel to depth;

☐   Sheathed internal partition required parallel to frontage:

☐   Sheathed internal partitions required parallel to both frontage and depth.

Where the wind charts require sheathed internal partitions, these must be provided in each dwelling of a terrace or detached pair. The partitions must be located in the ground storey within the middle thirds of the plan as shown in the accompanying diagram. The faces to be

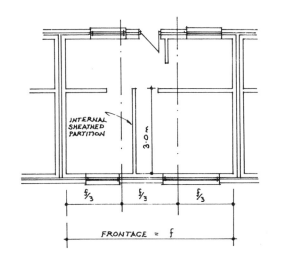

POSITIONS OF SHEATHED INTERNAL PARTITIONS WHEN REQUIRED FOR WIND BRACING

FOR EXAMPLE :—
8.4 m FRONTAGE X 5.4 m DEPTH
FROM WIND CHART 8

INTERNAL SHEATHED PARTITION

3.0

f/3   f/3   f/3

FRONTAGE = f

SIMILARLY SHEATHED INTERNAL PARTITIONS REQUIRED TO BRACE AGAINST WIND ON THE FLANK/GABLE WALLS MUST BE AT RIGHT ANGLES TO AND WITHIN THE MIDDLE THIRD ZONE OF SUCH WALLS

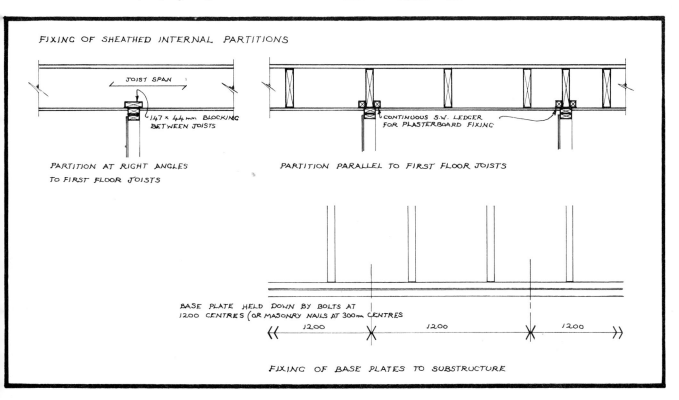

FIXING OF SHEATHED INTERNAL PARTITIONS

JOIST SPAN

147 x 44 mm BLOCKING BETWEEN JOISTS

PARTITION AT RIGHT ANGLES TO FIRST FLOOR JOISTS

CONTINUOUS S.W. LEDGER FOR PLASTERBOARD FIXING

PARTITION PARALLEL TO FIRST FLOOR JOISTS

BASE PLATE HELD DOWN BY BOLTS AT 1200 CENTRES (OR MASONRY NAILS AT 300mm CENTRES

1200   1200   1200

FIXING OF BASE PLATES TO SUBSTRUCTURE

sheathed should be marked on the final construction drawings. The sheathed partitions may be provided in two parts provided that each part is at least 1.800 m long.

Panels sheathed with plywood on one face are similar in construction to 'outside wall frames' (see page 19). Where panels are required to be sheathed on both faces, the fixing and layout specification for the additional plywood is the same. One face only should have factory applied sheathing to permit site fixing and inclusion of any services.

Sheathed internal partitions are fixed at the head as follows:

(a) *Partitions parallel to the joists.* Partitions must occur directly beneath a joist; to comply with this requirement an additional joist must be used if necessary. Head binders should be nailed to the top plate of the panel and the joist skew nailed to the head binder. All nails should be 3.75 mm diameter and 75 mm long spaced at 150 mm in the case of partitions ply sheathed on one face and 75 mm in the case of partitions ply sheathed on both faces, alternate fixings being on opposite sides of the joist. Noggings will be required for fixing plasterboard.

(b) *Partitions at right angles to the joists.* 147 × 44 mm blocking should be fixed between the joists immediately over the partition head and the same fixings as above should be used.

Sheathed internal partitions are fixed at the foot as follows:

(a) *Concrete ground slab.* The panel base plate should be nailed to the soleplate using the same fixing specification as given above for nailing the head binder to the panel top plate. The loose soleplate should be bolted to the substructure at 1200 mm centres using 12.7 mm diameter bolts, or, provided that the soleplate is solidly bedded into the full depth of the floor screed it may be fixed to the substructure by means of 4.0 mm diameter shot-fired or masonry nails at 300 mm centres, penetrating at least 25 mm into the concrete slab.

(b) *Suspended timber ground floor.* Partitions must occur directly above a joist or where partitions are at right angles to the joists blocking must be provided. The panel base plate should be fixed to the joist through the floor decking in the same manner as that detailed above for the head fixing.

It must be decided how the outside walls and separating walls can best be divided into individual frames. These must be not less than 1.800 metres, nor more than 3.600 metres long.

(iii) *Sketch external elevations*

The external elevations should now be sketched out to show the position and size of openings. Note that it is necessary to keep within the permissible percentages allowed for in the wind charts. Tables are included to assist in doing this. Reference to table 1 will quickly provide the areas of most commonly sized openings. By adding together the areas of openings in each storey for each elevation these totals can be compared with the maximum allowable values for each storey in table 2 for the given elevations so that the 20, 30 or 40 percentage figures will not be exceeded. For two storey houses the

Table 1 Areas of openings (m²)

		width of opening (m)						
		0.3	0.6	0.9	1.2	1.5	1.8	2.1
	0.3	0.09	0.18	0.27	0.36	0.45	0.54	0.63
	0.45	0.14	0.27	0.41	0.54	0.68	0.81	0.95
	0.6	0.18	0.36	0.54	0.72	0.90	1.08	1.26
	0.75	0.23	0.45	0.68	0.90	1.13	1.35	1.58
	0.9	0.27	0.54	0.81	1.08	1.35	1.62	1.89
height of	1.05	0.32	0.63	0.95	1.26	1.58	1.89	2.21
opening (m)	1.2	0.36	0.72	1.08	1.44	1.80	2.16	2.52
	1.35	0.41	0.81	1.22	1.62	2.03	2.43	2.84
	1.5	0.45	0.90	1.35	1.80	2.25	2.70	3.15
	1.65	0.50	0.99	1.49	1.98	2.48	2.97	3.47
	1.8	0.54	1.08	1.62	2.16	2.70	3.24	3.78
	1.95	0.59	1.17	1.76	2.34	2.93	3.51	4.10
	2.1	0.63	1.26	1.89	2.52	3.15	3.78	4.41

Table 2 Permissible total areas of openings in external walls (m²)

length of wall (m)	percentage openings permitted in each storey		
	20%	30%	40%
3.6	1.73	2.59	3.46
3.9	1.87	2.81	3.74
4.2	2.02	3.02	4.03
4.5	2.16	3.24	4.32
4.8	3.20	3.46	4.61
5.1	2.45	3.67	4.90
5.4	2.59	3.89	5.18
5.7	2.74	4.10	5.47
6.0	2.88	4.32	5.76
6.3	3.02	4.54	6.05
6.6	3.17	4.75	6.34
6.0	3.31	4.97	6.62
7.2	3.46	5.18	6.91
7.5	3.60	5.40	7.20
7.8	3.74	5.62	7.49
8.1	3.89	5.83	7.78
8.4	4.03	6.05	8.05
8.7	4.18	6.26	8.35
9.0	4.32	6.48	8.64
9.3	4.46	6.70	8.93
9.6	4.61	6.91	9.22
9.9	5.75	7.13	9.50
10.2	4.90	7.34	9.79
10.8	5.18	7.78	10.4
11.4	5.47	8.21	10.9
12.0	5.76	8.64	11.5
12.6	6.05	9.07	12.1
13.2	6.34	9.50	12.7
13.8	6.62	9.94	13.3
14.4	6.91	10.4	13.8
15.0	7.20	10.8	14.4
15.6	7.49	11.2	15.0
16.2	7.78	11.7	15.6

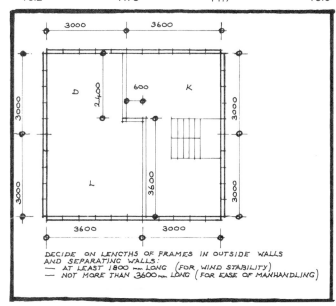

DECIDE ON LENGTHS OF FRAMES IN OUTSIDE WALLS AND SEPARATING WALLS:
— AT LEAST 1800 mm LONG (FOR WIND STABILITY)
— NOT MORE THAN 3600 mm LONG (FOR EASE OF MANHANDLING)

ground floor walls should be checked as described. The first floor openings can then normally be checked merely by inspection.

The rules for openings in external walls are as follows:

(a) keep all openings at least 300 mm from the ends of frames, and from any other opening in the same frame;

(b) do not use openings more than 2.100 metres wide;

(c) with main openings, keep the head 2.100 metres above floor level;

(d) in two storey dwellings, avoid 'staggered' first floor openings above ground floor openings more than 1.500 metres wide;

(e) as far as possible fit any small openings between the studs. Then no lintel will be needed.

3 Complete the design

(i) Incorporate preferred stairwell

Stairwell dimensions are given on page 23. Trimmers and trimming joists are shown on page 54 Trimmers and trimming joists to be as shown in the diagrams.

(ii) Select wall studs

All studs to be 97 x 44 mm GS grade except for external wall studs in the C2 and B2 wind categories which are to be 97 x 44 mm SS grade. Studs in internally sheathed partitions which do not support floor joists may be 72 x 44 mm GS grade.

(iii) Select lintels and cripple studs

Lintels over clear openings up to and including 1500 mm to be pairs of 47 x 219 mm SS grade timbers fixed together. Lintels over clear openings greater than 1500 mm and up to 2100 mm carrying floor load only to be pairs of 47 x 219 mm SS grade timbers fixed together. Lintels over clear openings greater than 1500 mm and up to 2100 mm carrying roof load or roof plus floor loads to be 94 x 219 mm 65 grade hardwood, as specified in Chapter 2.3.

Single cripple studs are to be used throughout except for the 2100 mm openings when two are required.

(iv) Select floor joists

Maximum clear spans in metres of ground and first floor joists at 600 mm spacings are given in the following tables:

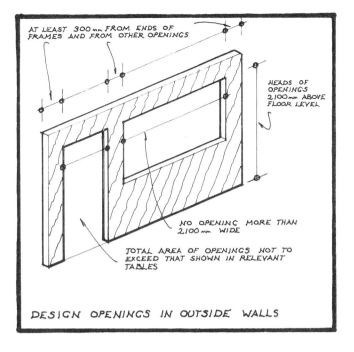

DESIGN OPENINGS IN OUTSIDE WALLS

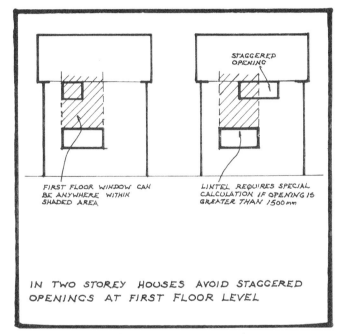

IN TWO STOREY HOUSES AVOID STAGGERED OPENINGS AT FIRST FLOOR LEVEL

Ground floor joists

Grade of Timber	Depth of Joist (mm)	Breadth of Joist (mm)		
		38	47	63
		maximum clear span in metres (600 mm joist spacings)		
GS	145	1.84 (1.8)	2.06 (1.8)	2.40 (2.4)
	169	2.16 (2.1)	2.42 (2.4)	2.81 (2.7)
SS	194	2.50 (2.4)	2.79 (2.7)	3.24 (3.0)
	219	3.41 (3.3)	3.60 (3.6)	3.90 (3.9)

First floor joists

Grade of Timber	Depth of Joist (mm)	Breadth of Joist (mm)		
		38	47	63
		maximum clear span in metres (600 mm joist spacings)		
GS	194	2.72 (2.7)	3.04 (3.0)	3.53 (3.3)
SS	219	3.56 (3.3)	3.76 (3.6)	4.05 (3.9)

(Figures in brackets are the highest permissible dimensions which are multiples of 300 mm).

STRAIGHT FLIGHT STAIR   DOG-LEGGED STAIR

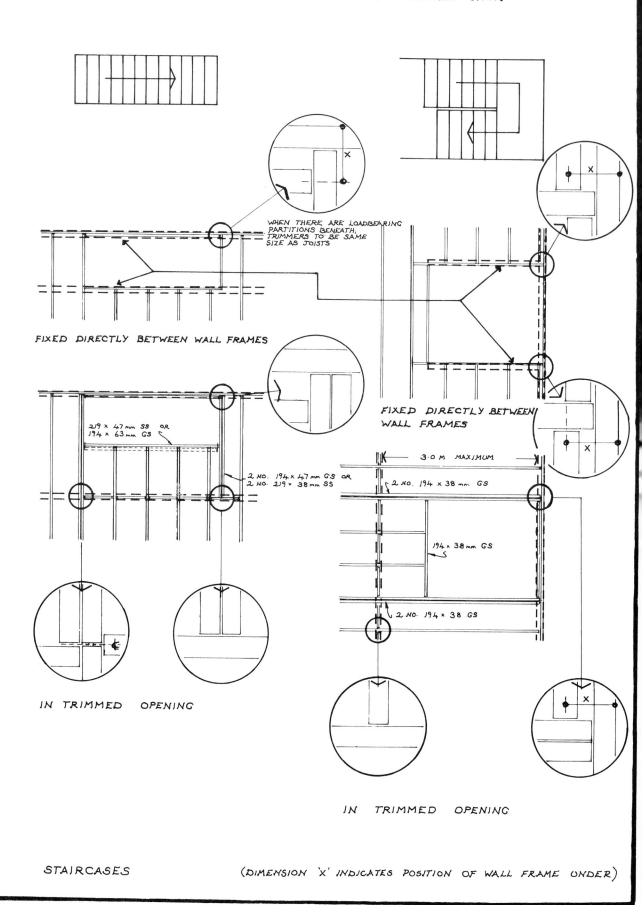

WHEN THERE ARE LOADBEARING
PARTITIONS BENEATH,
TRIMMERS TO BE SAME
SIZE AS JOISTS

FIXED DIRECTLY BETWEEN WALL FRAMES

219 × 47 mm SS OR
194 × 63 mm GS

2 NO. 194 × 47 mm GS OR
2 NO. 219 × 38 mm SS

FIXED DIRECTLY BETWEEN
WALL FRAMES

3·0 M MAXIMUM

2 NO. 194 × 38 mm GS

194 × 38 mm GS

2 NO. 194 × 38 GS

IN TRIMMED OPENING

IN TRIMMED OPENING

STAIRCASES   (DIMENSION 'X' INDICATES POSITION OF WALL FRAME UNDER)

WIND ZONE MAP

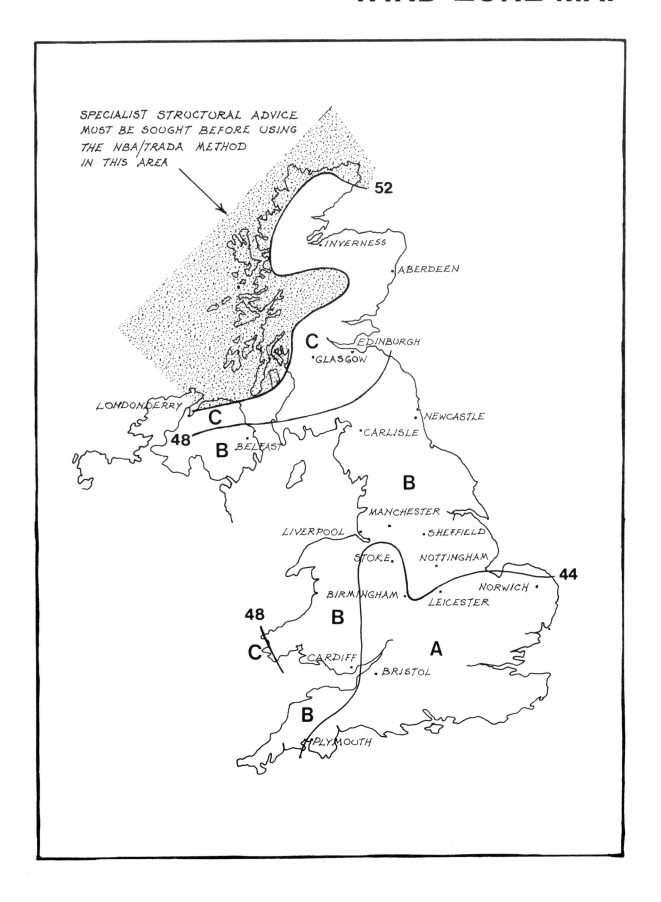

SPECIALIST STRUCTURAL ADVICE
MUST BE SOUGHT BEFORE USING
THE NBA/TRADA METHOD
IN THIS AREA

WIND CHART 1

2 STOREY ~ WIND ZONES A3,A4 22½°-30° PITCH ROOF

Limitation for 40% openings in external walls (front and back)

frontage

Limitation for 30% openings in external walls (front and back)

Gable walls of houses are generally assumed to have openings not exceeding 20% of the walls

Indicates dwellings that can be built as detached units with 30% openings in the gable wall when additional internal wall sheathing is provided (see chapter 2.1 1(ii))

No internal partition required

I Sheathed internal partitions required parallel to depth (gable) (see chapter 2.1 2(ii))

— Sheathed internal partitions required parallel to frontage (see chapter 2.1 2(ii))

WIND CHART 2

2 STOREY ~ WIND ZONE A2
22½°~30° PITCH ROOF

Limitation for 40% openings in external walls (front and back)

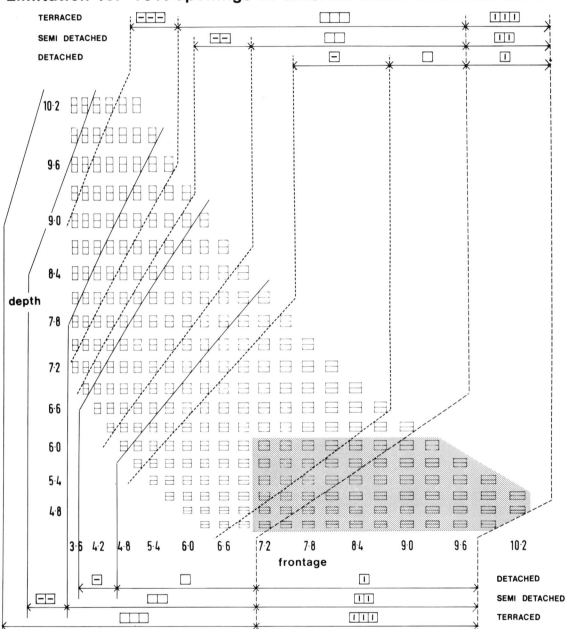

Limitation for 30% openings in external walls (front and back)

Gable walls of houses are generally assumed to have openings not exceeding 20% of the walls

▨ Indicates dwellings that can be built as detached units with 30% openings in the gable wall when additional internal wall sheathing is provided (see chapter 2.1 1(ii))

☐ No internal partition required

[I] Sheathed internal partitions required parallel to depth (gable) (see chapter 2.1 2(ii))

[—] Sheathed internal partitions required parallel to frontage (see chapter 2.1 2(ii))

2 STOREY ~ WIND ZONES B3,B4
22½°~30° PITCH ROOF

Limitation for 40% openings in external walls (front and back)

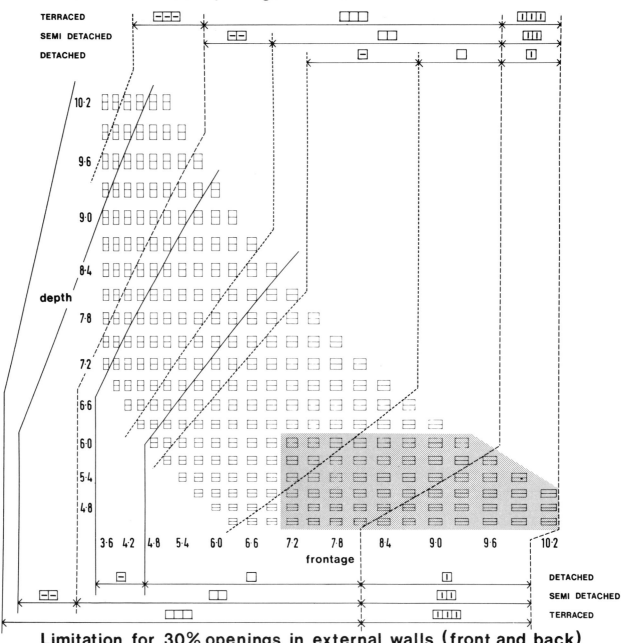

Limitation for 30% openings in external walls (front and back)

Gable walls of houses are generally assumed to have openings not exceeding 20% of the walls

Indicates dwellings that can be built as detached units with 30% openings in the gable wall when additional internal wall sheathing is provided (see chapter 2.1 1(ii))

No internal partition required

Sheathed internal partitions required parallel to depth (gable) (see chapter 2.1 2(ii))

Sheathed internal partitions required parallel to frontage (see chapter 2.1 2(ii))

WIND CHART 4

2 STOREY ~ WIND ZONE B2
22½°~30° PITCH ROOF

Limitation for 40% openings in external walls (front and back)

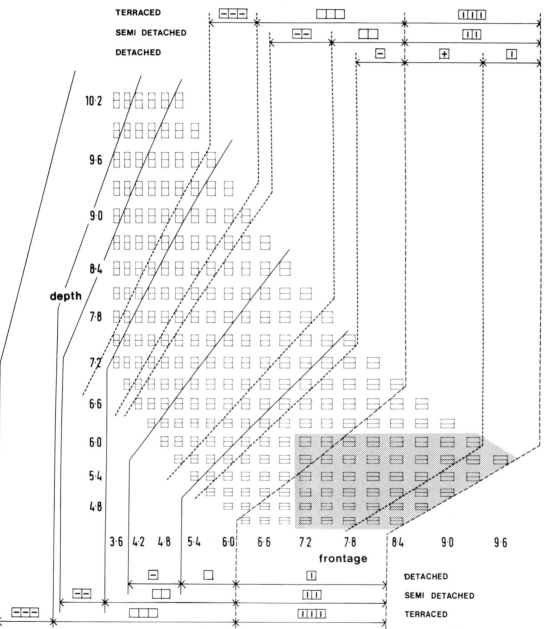

Limitation for 30% openings in external walls (front and back)

Gable walls of houses are generally assumed to have openings not exceeding 20% of the walls

Indicates dwellings that can be built as detached units with 30% openings in the gable wall when additional internal wall sheathing is provided (see chapter 2.1 1 (ii))

☐ No internal partition required

I Sheathed internal partitions required parallel to depth (gable) (see chapter 2.1 2 (ii))

— Sheathed internal partitions required parallel to frontage (see chapter 2.1 2 (ii))

+ Sheathed internal partitions required in both directions (see chapter 2.1 2 (ii))

2 STOREY ~ WIND ZONES C3,C4
22½°~30° PITCH ROOF

Limitation for 40% openings in external walls (front and back)

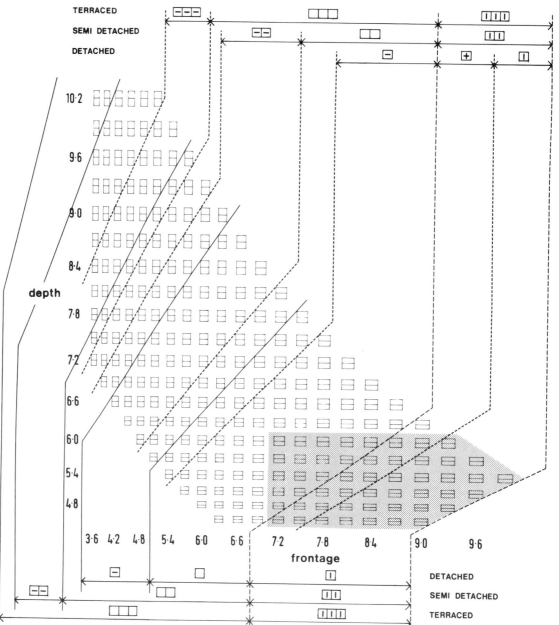

frontage

Limitation for 30% openings in external walls (front and back)

Gable walls of houses are generally assumed to have openings not exceeding 20% of the walls

Indicates dwellings that can be built as detached units with 30% openings in the gable wall when additional internal wall sheathing is provided (see chapter 2.1 1(ii))

No internal partition required

I — Sheathed internal partitions required parallel to depth (gable) (see chapter 2.1 2(ii))

— — Sheathed internal partitions required parallel to frontage (see chapter 2.1 2(ii))

+ — Sheathed internal partitions required in both directions (see chapter 2.1 2(ii))

2 STOREY ~ WIND ZONE C2
22½°~30° PITCH ROOF

Limitation for 40% openings in external walls (front and back)

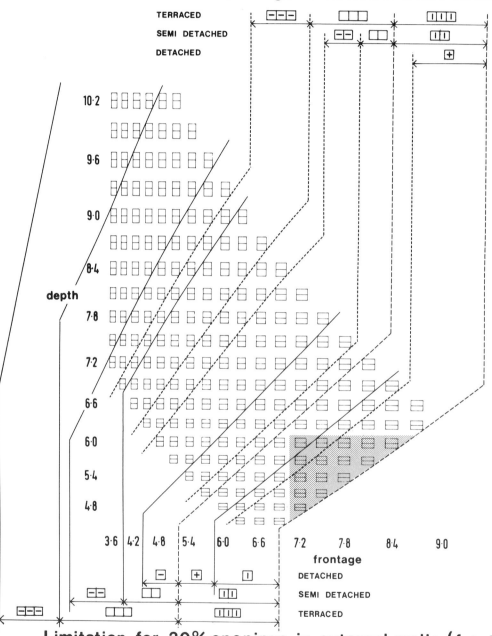

Limitation for 30% openings in external walls (front and back)

Gable walls of houses are generally assumed to have openings not exceeding 20% of the walls

Indicates dwellings that can be built as detached units with 30% openings in the gable wall when additional internal wall sheathing is provided (see chapter 2.1 1 (ii))

No internal partition required

| I | Sheathed internal partitions required parallel to depth (gable) (see chapter 2.1 2 (ii))

− Sheathed internal partitions required parallel to frontage (see chapter 2.1 2 (ii))

+ Sheathed internal partitions required in both directions (see chapter 2.1 2 (ii))

2 STOREY ~ WIND ZONES A3, A4
35°~40° PITCH ROOF

Limitation for 40% openings in external walls (front and back)

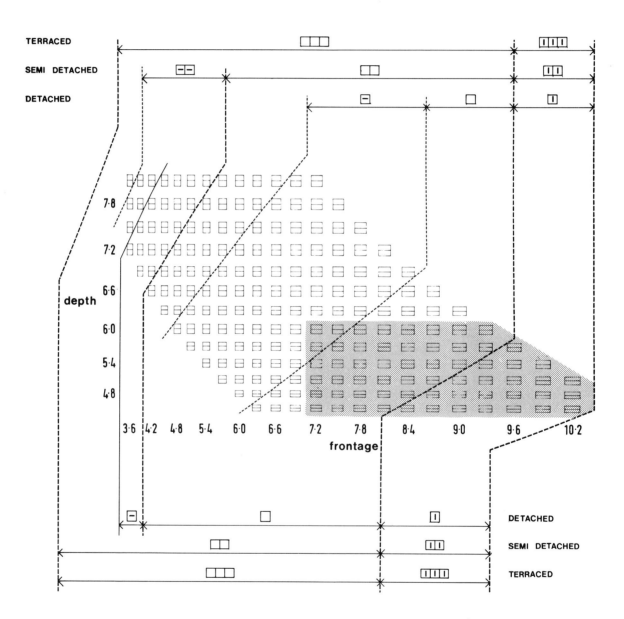

Limitation for 30% openings in external walls (front and back)

Gable walls of houses are generally assumed to have openings not exceeding 20% of the walls

Indicates dwellings that can be built as detached units with 30% openings in the gable wall when additional internal wall sheathing is provided (see chapter 2.1 1(ii))

No internal partition required

I Sheathed internal partitions required parallel to depth (gable) (see chapter 2.1 2(ii))

— Sheathed internal partitions required parallel to frontage (see chapter 2.1 2(ii))

WIND CHART 8

2 STOREY ~ WIND ZONE A2
35°~40° PITCH ROOF

Limitation for 40% openings in external walls (front and back)

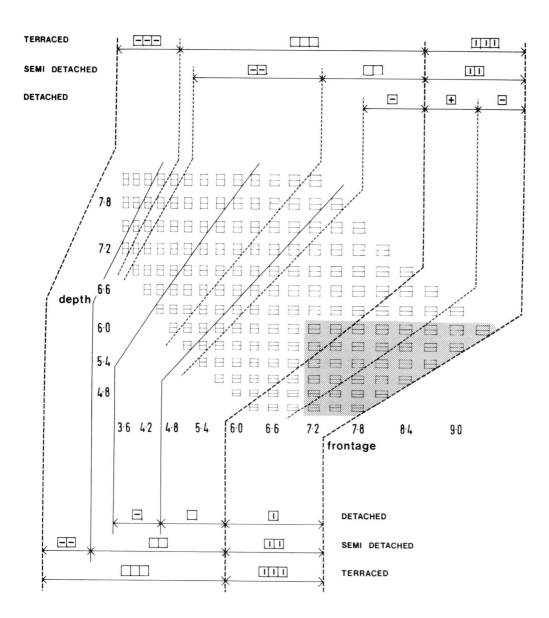

Limitation for 30% openings in external walls (front and back)

Gable walls of houses are generally assumed to have openings not exceeding 20% of the walls

Indicates dwellings that can be built as detached units with 30% openings in the gable wall when additional internal wall sheathing is provided (see chapter 2.1 1(ii))

No internal partition required

| Sheathed internal partitions required parallel to depth (gable) (see chapter 2.1 2(ii))

— Sheathed internal partitions required parallel to frontage (see chapter 2.1 2(ii))

+ Sheathed internal partitions required in both directions (see chapter 2.1 2(ii))

2 STOREY ~ WIND ZONES B3,B4
35°~40° PITCH ROOF

Limitation for 40% openings in external walls (front and back)

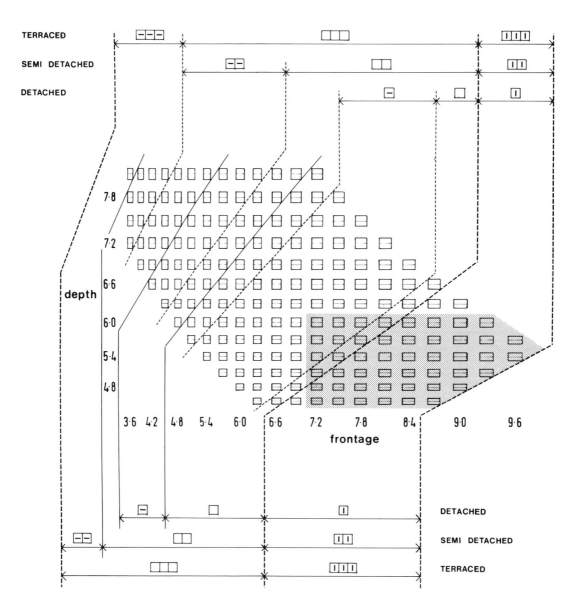

Limitation for 30% openings in external walls (front and back)

Gable walls of houses are generally assumed to have openings not exceeding 20% of the walls

☐ Indicates dwellings that can be built as detached units with 30% openings in the gable wall when additional internal wall sheathing is provided (see chapter 2.1 1(ii))

☐ No internal partition required

│ Sheathed internal partitions required parallel to depth (gable) (see chapter 2.1 2(ii))

─ Sheathed internal partitions required parallel to frontage (see chapter 2.1 2(ii))

2 STOREY ~ WIND ZONE B2
35°~40° PITCH ROOF

Limitation for 40% openings in external walls (front and back)

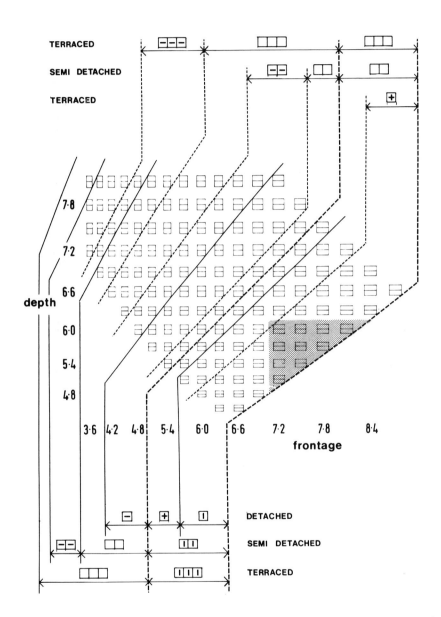

Limitation for 30% openings in external walls (front and back)

Gable walls of houses are generally assumed to have openings not exceeding 20% of the walls

▦ Indicates dwellings that can be built as detached units with 30% openings in the gable wall when additional internal wall sheathing is provided (see chapter 2.1 1 (ii))

☐ No internal partition required

|I| Sheathed internal partitions required parallel to depth (gable) (see chapter 2.1 2 (ii))

|−| Sheathed internal partitions required parallel to frontage (see chapter 2.1 2 (ii))

|+| Sheathed internal partitions required in both directions (see chapter 2.1 2 (ii))

2 STOREY ~ WIND ZONES C3,C4 35°~40° PITCH ROOF

Limitation for 40% openings in external walls (front and back)

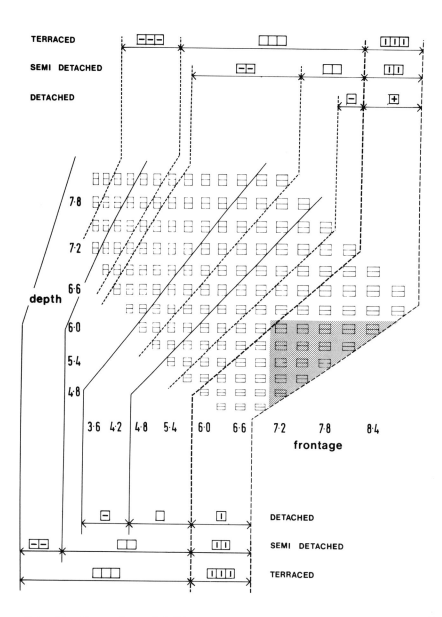

Limitation for 30% openings in external walls (front and back)

Gable walls of houses are generally assumed to have openings not exceeding 20% of the walls

▨   Indicates dwellings that can be built as detached units with 30% openings in the gable wall when additional internal wall sheathing is provided (see chapter 2.1 1(ii))

☐   No internal partition required

|I| Sheathed internal partitions required parallel to depth (gable) (see chapter 2.1 2(ii))

|—| Sheathed internal partitions required parallel to frontage (see chapter 2.1 2(ii))

|+| Sheathed internal partitions required in both directions (see chapter 2.1 2(ii))

2 STOREY ~ WIND ZONE C2
35°~40° PITCH ROOF

Limitation for 40% openings in external walls (front and back)

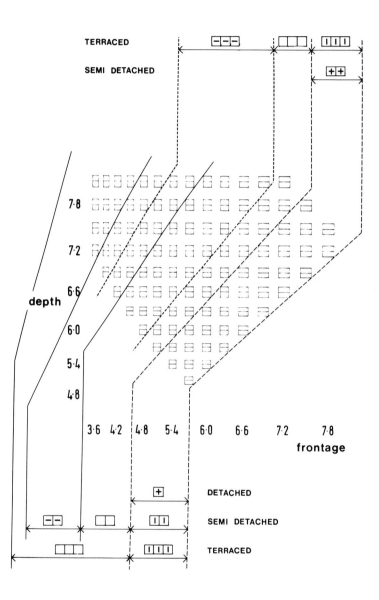

TERRACED

SEMI DETACHED

depth

7·8

7·2

6·6

6·0

5·4

4·8

3·6 4·2 4·8 5·4 6·0 6·6 7·2 7·8

frontage

DETACHED

SEMI DETACHED

TERRACED

Limitation for 30% openings in external walls (front and back)

Gable walls of houses are generally assumed to have openings not exceeding 20% of the walls

Indicates dwellings that can be built as detached units with 30% openings in the gable wall when additional internal wall sheathing is provided (see chapter 2.1 1 (ii))

No internal partition required

I Sheathed internal partitions required parallel to depth (gable) (see chapter 2.1 2 (ii))

– Sheathed internal partitions required parallel to frontage (see chapter 2.1 2 (ii))

+ Sheathed internal partitions required in both directions (see chapter 2.1 2 (ii))

ONE STOREY ~ ALL WIND ZONES
22½°~ 30° PITCH ROOF

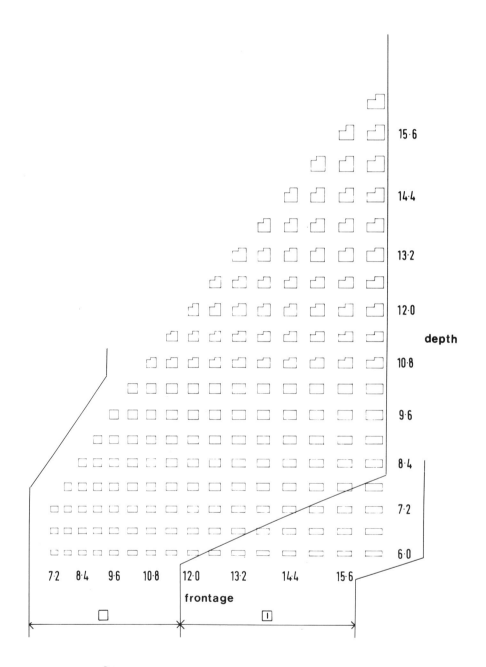

depth

15·6

14·4

13·2

12·0

10·8

9·6

8·4

7·2

6·0

7·2   8·4   9·6   10·8   12·0   13·2   14·4   15·6

frontage

Limitations for 30% openings in all external walls

☐   No internal partition required

Ⅰ   Sheathed internal partitions required parallel to depth (see chapter 2.1 2(ii))

WIND CHART 14

ONE STOREY ~ WIND ZONES A3, A4 35°~40° PITCH ROOF

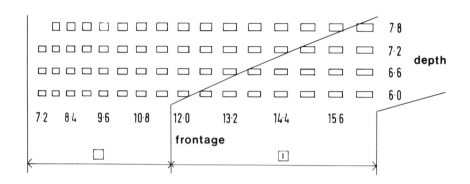

Limitations for 30% openings in all external walls

WIND CHART 15

ONE STOREY ~ WIND ZONES A2, B3, B4 35°~40° PITCH ROOF

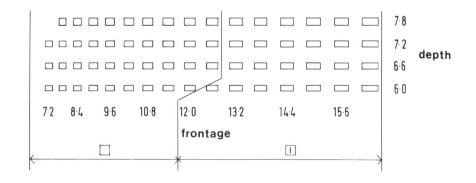

Limitations for 30% openings in all external walls

☐ No internal partition required

[I] Sheathed internal partitions required parallel to depth (see chapter 2.1 2(ii))

ONE STOREY ~ WIND ZONES B2,C3,C4
35°~40° PITCH ROOF

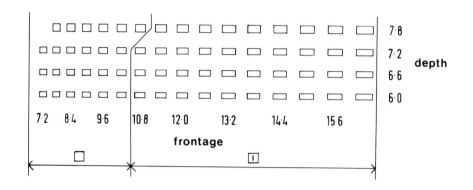

Limitations for 30% openings in all external walls

WIND CHART 17

ONE STOREY ~ WIND ZONE C2
35°~40° PITCH ROOF

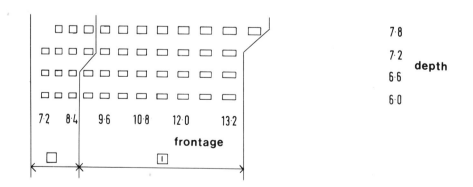

Limitations for 30% openings in all external walls

☐ No internal partition required

Ⅰ Sheathed internal partitions required parallel to depth (see chapter 2.1 2(ii))

Drawings Needed

Drawings will be needed of the timber structure of the dwelling. They will be required not only to finalise details of the construction, but also for ordering materials, making up panels (whether on site or in the factory), and for site erection.

The set of drawings required

The following list gives the typical set of drawings needed to make and erect the timber superstructure, and what has to be shown on each one. A scale of 1:50 should be used. It is best to use basic dimensions throughout for panels and other pieces (usually multiples of 100 mm) on the drawings.

(1a) Ground floor base plate layout

Base plates (required under all loadbearing frames), showing the location of holding down straps or nails, and the dimensions needed for setting them out accurately on site

or

(1b) Suspended timber ground floor layout

Location of foundation walls.

Wall plates, showing the location of holding down straps or nails.

Normal joists at 600 mm centres, showing lengths and sections needed.

Perimeter joists.

Extra joists under non-loadbearing partitions parallel to normal joists.

Strutting.

Blocking.

Locations and requirements of any joist hangers and straps.

Floor decking layout if chipboard or plywood is used.

(2) Ground floor panel layout

Panels, showing openings, normal studs and cripple studs.

Sheathing.

Extra studs needed at corners and other junctions.

Extra noggings for fixtures and fittings.

(3) First floor joist layout

Outline of head binders carrying joists.

Normal joists at 600 mm centres, showing lengths and

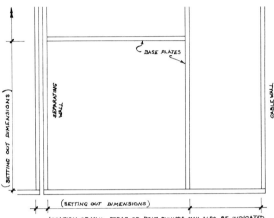

GROUND FLOOR BASE PLATE LAYOUT

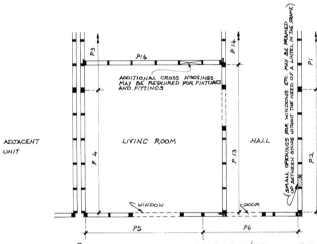

GROUND FLOOR PANEL LAYOUT

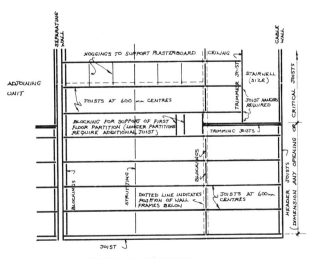

FIRST FLOOR JOIST LAYOUT

Illustrations not to scale.

sections needed.

Extra joists under partitions parallel to normal joists.

Trimming round stairs, lengths and sections, and fixings.

Perimeter header joists.

Strutting.

Blocking over loadbearing partitions.

Location and requirements of any joist hangers and straps.

Noggings to support free edges of ceiling linings.

Floor decking layout if chipboard or plywood is used.

(4) First floor panel layout

(similar to ground floor (1b)).

(5) Roof truss layout

Outline of head binders carrying rafters.

Outline of spandrel panels carrying verge ladders and separating wall rafters.

Layout of trussed rafters.

Bracing to roof structure (diagonal bracing under rafters, ridge binders and binders on top of ceiling ties).

Barge boards.

Eaves fascias.

Tank platform.

Nogging for fixing of ceiling linings.

(6) Elevations of all perimeter framing
(external walling and separating walls) and loadbearing partitions.

Openings, including full information on lintels and cripple studs.

Panels, showing all studs.

Sheathing required on panels showing layout of sheets.

Diagonal bracing of separating wall panels.

Additional studs at external corners and other junctions.

Head binders.

Perimeter joists.

Spandrel panels.

Verge ladders, and separating wall rafters.

Setting out of trussed rafters on to head binders.

Coding of factory-made panels

It must be possible to identify panels easily and quickly in the factory and on site. Simple numbering can be used on small contracts.

This coding should be marked up on drawings, and stamped on each panel in the factory.

Letters can be added to show where panels belong, such as GF7 (Ground floor panel No. 7).

On sites where there are 'handed' houses, make sure that the coding sorts out clearly any handed panels.

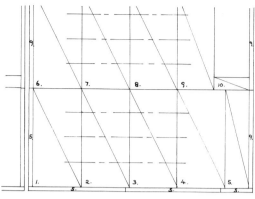

SHEET SIZE : PLYWOOD — 2400 x 1200mm (T & G ON LONG EDGE)
CHIPBOARD — 2400 x 600mm (T & G ON ALL EDGES)

SHEETS TO BE LAID AT RIGHT ANGLES TO THE FLOOR JOISTS AND ALL CUT EDGES TO BE SUPPORTED ON NOGGINGS OR BLOCKINGS. IF DECKING IS LAID AFTER FIRST FLOOR PARTITIONS, A PACK OF THE SAME DEPTH AS THE DECKING WILL BE REQUIRED UNDER WALL FRAMES AND ADDITIONAL BLOCKING AND NOGGING WILL BE NEEDED TO SUPPORT THE DECKING AT ROOM PERIMETERS

FIRST FLOOR DECKING LAYOUT

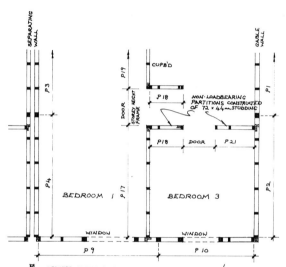

▨ — DENOTES LOCATION OF ADDITIONAL STUDS FOR PANEL/PLASTERBOARD FIXING

LOCATION AND SIZE OF WINDOW AND DOOR OPENINGS REQUIRE DIMENSIONING ESPECIALLY IF ONE SIDE DOES NOT LINE UP WITH THE 600mm SPACING OF THE STUDS

FIRST FLOOR PANEL LAYOUT

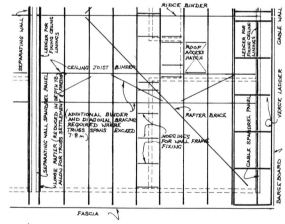

(ANY FRAMING REQUIRED FOR WATER STORAGE TANKS SHOULD ALSO BE SHOWN ON THIS DRAWING)

ROOF TRUSS LAYOUT

Illustrations not to scale.

72

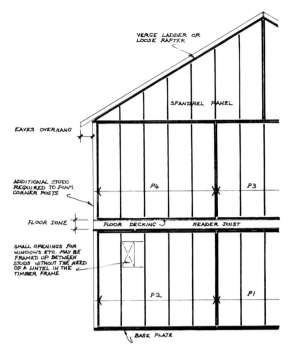

VERGE LADDER OR LOOSE RAFTER

SPANDREL PANEL

EAVES OVERHANG

ADDITIONAL STUDS REQUIRED TO FORM CORNER POSTS

P4   P3

FLOOR ZONE

FLOOR DECKING   HEADER JOIST

SMALL OPENINGS FOR WINDOWS ETC. MAY BE FRAMED UP BETWEEN STUDS WITHOUT THE NEED OF A LINTEL IN THE TIMBER FRAME

P2   P1

BASE PLATE

GABLE WALL: ALL WALL FRAMES AND SPANDRELS TO BE SHEATHED ON THEIR EXTERNAL FACE

SEPARATING WALL: ALL WALL FRAMES TO HAVE DIAGONAL BRACING TO THE CAVITY SIDE OF THE PANEL

GABLE OR SEPARATING WALL ELEVATION

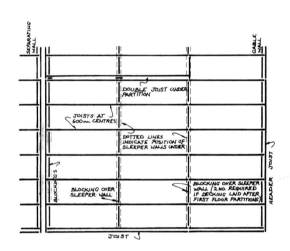

SEPARATING WALL SPANDREL PANEL   GABLE WALL SPANDREL PANEL

ROOF TRUSSES AT 600mm CENTRES

HEAD BINDER

WINDOW   WINDOW

ADDITIONAL STUDS TO FORM CORNER POSTS

P9   P10

FLOOR ZONE   FLOOR DECKING   JOISTS

HEAD BINDER

LINTEL

WINDOW   DOOR

P5   P6

BASE PLATE

DIAGONAL LINES INDICATE SHEATHING REQUIREMENTS TO THE EXTERNAL FACE OF THE WALL PANELS

LOCATION AND SIZE OF WINDOW AND DOOR OPENINGS REQUIRE DIMENSIONING ESPECIALLY IF ONE SIDE DOES NOT LINE UP WITH THE 600mm SPACING OF STUDS

FRONT ELEVATION

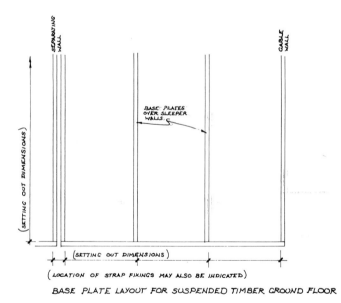

SEPARATING WALL   GABLE WALL

(SETTING OUT DIMENSIONS)

BASE PLATES OVER SLEEPER WALLS

(SETTING OUT DIMENSIONS)

(LOCATION OF STRAP FIXINGS MAY ALSO BE INDICATED)

BASE PLATE LAYOUT FOR SUSPENDED TIMBER GROUND FLOOR

SEPARATING WALL   GABLE WALL

DOUBLE JOIST UNDER PARTITION

JOISTS AT 600mm CENTRES

DOTTED LINES INDICATE POSITION OF SLEEPER WALLS UNDER

BLOCKINGS

BLOCKING OVER SLEEPER WALL

BLOCKING OVER SLEEPER WALL (2 NO. REQUIRED IF DECKING LAID AFTER FIRST FLOOR PARTITIONS)

HEADER JOIST

JOIST

JOIST LAYOUT - SUSPENDED TIMBER GROUND FLOOR

Illustrations not to scale.

What to Specify or Order

Softwood

Species:

All of the following species are suitable. Stocks vary, so it is best to allow the supplier a choice from within this list. The origin of each species is shown in the list.

Redwood	Imported
Whitewood	Imported
American pitch pine	Imported
Western hemlock	Imported
Caribbean pitch pine	Imported
Douglas fir	Home grown or imported
European larch	Home grown
Japanese larch	Home grown
Scots pine	Home grown

Grade:

All structural pieces must be stress graded. (But note that this is not needed for non-structural pieces such as noggings and cavity barriers).

SS grade (Special Structural) is used for 219 mm deep pieces used for long-span joists and lintels.

GS grade (General Structural) is used for all other structural pieces. These grades are taken from BS 4978: 1973. 'Timber grades for structural softwood'. Note that these are grades resulting from *visual* inspection. Every piece must carry a grade stamp. If this mark is removed during machining, then the piece must be restamped. Note also that the standard allows the equivalent machine grades to be supplied where visual grades are specified. Thus MGS grade may be supplied instead of GS, and MSS instead of SS.

Using graded softwood. Pieces must be selected and cut so that no defects allowed by the grading reduces the strength of frames at joints, or the adequate fixing of linings and floorings.

Moisture content of softwood and hardwood should not be more than 20 per cent.

Range of sections

The range of softwood sections used in this Manual are set out in the table below. Tolerances are those of BS 4471: Part 1: 1978.

Preservative treatment

Base plates must always be preservative treated. So must cavity closers and any battens applied to the structure outside the breather paper.

Whether or not the rest of the softwood is treated is optional. If correctly built, the timber structure will remain relatively dry, and well below the danger limit at which

Range of softwood sections.

Basic Sawn Size	Machine Planing	Finished Size	Stress Grade if structural	Use
47 × 47	processed	44 × 44	—	noggings
75 × 47	processed	72 × 44	—	all internal non-loadbearing partitions
100 × 25	processed	97 × 22 (or as depth of floor decking)	GS	packers under wall frames at decking level, bracing in separating walls and roofs
100 × 47	processed	97 × 44	GS (SS in special circumstances)	wall framing, head binders, verge ladders, rafters at separating walls
100 × 63	processed	97 × 60	GS	base plates, wall plates
150 × 38 47 & 63	regularised	145 × 38 47 & 63	GS	short span floor joists in ground floors
150 × 38	—	150 × 38		strutting joists spanning more than 2.500 metres
200 × 38 47 & 63	regularised	194 × 38 47 & 63	GS	upper floor joists
225 × 38 47 & 63	regularised	219 × 38 47 & 63	SS	long span joists, lintels

fungal or insect attack can normally start. On the other hand it should be noted that in timber frame housing preservative treatment of softwood is being used increasingly. This is largely because it gives an added assurance of durability, both to housing committees in the public sector, and to house purchasers and building societies in the private sector.

Suppliers should as far as possible be allowed the option to use any one of the methods recommended in BS 5268: Part 5: 1976 'Preservative treatment for construction timbers'.

It is usually necessary for preservative to be brush applied to the ends of any pieces cut after treatment. This is because the treatment may not penetrate into the core of the pieces. Check this matter with the supplier.

Note that in some areas in south-east England, as with traditional construction, trussed rafters require treatment. This is required in the Building Regulations Part B where roofs are liable to attack by the house longhorn beetle. Treatment in these areas must be given also to all other pieces in the roof space, such as spandrel panels, diagonal braces, noggings, etc.

Hardwood

Structural hardwood is used for lintels over wide openings. Any of the species in the list below is suitable. Pieces should be stress graded, and must be 65 grade or better to CP 112: Part 2: Appendix A.

Keruing, kapur, jarrah, kempas, karri, balau, opepe, ekki, okan or celtis.

Sheathing for external and selected internal panels

Plywood

8 mm exterior grade Douglas fir plywood must be used. This can be *either*

unsanded sheathing to Canadian Standard 0121, or

C/C exterior grade to American Plywood Association Standard P1/74.

Tempered hardboard

Tempered hardboard must comply with the requirements of BS 1142: Part 2: 1971 and must not be less than 6.4 mm thick. It must be cured in accordance with manufacturer's instructions before being fixed to wall frames.

High density medium board or panelboard

Medium board must comply with the requirements of BS 1142: Part 2: 1971 and must not be less than 9 mm thick. It must be cured in accordance with manufacturer's instructions before being fixed to wall frames.

Breather paper

This must be to BS 4016:1966.

Vapour barrier

Polyethylene sheeting not less than 250 gauge or aluminium foil backing to plasterboard.

Quilt cavity barriers

50×600 mm wire reinforced mineral quilt mattress — density not less than 80–90 kg/m³.

Insulation

Suspended timber ground floors, external walls and roofs: 100×600 mm mineral or glass wool quilt – density 12–20 kg/m³.

Separating wall: 600 mm mineral or glass wool quilt— density 12–20 kg/m³, min. thickness 25 mm.

Trussed rafters

The design of the trussed rafter is usually left to the supplier. It is sufficient to indicate that the trusses must comply with CP 112: Part 3: 1973.

The supplier will need to know the following:

(1) The spacing of trusses (which will be 600 mm).

(2) The pitch of the roof.

(3) The distance between the intersection points of the lower edges of rafters and ceiling ties. (This should be 250 mm more than the internal span between the wall frames carrying the rafters. This allows a suitable erection tolerance).

(4) The distance between the outer face of the wall plate and the intersection point (28 mm).

(5) The clear span between the wall frames.

(6) The eaves overhang, that is the horizontal distance between the intersection point as in (3) and the ends of the rafters at the eaves.

(7) The precise type of roofing finish to be used and its weight per m².

(8) The dimensions and positions of any chimneys or hatches.

(9) Full details of any water tanks to be carried by the ceiling ties. (It is usually best for such tanks to be carried on partitions at some suitable point in the dwelling).

(10) Details of preservative treatment, if any required.

Floorings

Any of the following are suitable:

(1) Tongued and grooved softwood boarding to BS 1297:1970, 21 mm finished thickness.

(2) Chipboard, tongued and grooved on all edges, 22 mm thick, which meets the requirements of BS 5669:1979 for domestic floorings in sheet sizes of 2400 mm x 600 mm. If the flooring is laid before the dwelling is weathertight the chipboard specified must be of a suitable moisture resistant quality.

(3) Plywood, tongued and grooved on long edges, 19 mm exterior grade Douglas fir Good One Side (G1S) to Canadian Standards CSA 0121 or CSA 0151 in sheet sizes 2400 x 1200 mm.

Plasterboard

12.7 mm tapered edge boards in sheets 2400 x 1200 mm, should conform to BS 1230:1970. Nails and other materials should conform to the manufacturers' specifications.

Nails and fixings

Nails used for the framing and its assembly on site should

conform to BS 1202: Part 1: 1974. Sizes should be as specified in Chapter 1.2 of this Manual.

Wall ties

Stainless steel or galvanised mild steel with a zinc coating of not less than 260g/m^2 as specified in BS 1243:1978 or flexible plastic wall ties holding an applicable Agrément Certificate are suitable.

Joist hangers

Should be used in accordance with manufacturers' recommendations. Protective coatings should conform with the relevant British Standards.

Dpc's

All damp-proof courses including those around windows should conform with BS 743:1970.

Metal lintels

Galvanised mild steel angle or proprietary metal lintels may be used conforming with BS 449: Part 2: 1969 and BS 729:1971. Proprietary metal lintels should hold an Agrément Certificate.

Ordering Factory-Made Frames

Fabrication

The methods in this Manual are quite suitable for framing made up on site. The site slab, if already poured, can form a clean level base for the work.

Work can be speeded up if framing pieces, such as studs and joists, are delivered to site already accurately precut by the supplier. Most timber frame houses in the UK are built, however, with factory made panels. In both cases, unless cranes are to be used on site, the storey-height panels should be kept to a length of not more than 3.600 metres. This is about the largest panel which can be put up on site easily by 3 men.

Ordering from panel suppliers

TRADA regional officers can supply names and addresses of suitable companies in the area of the site. Companies will need to have a set of drawings of the structure, as set out in Chapter 2.2 and it will also help them to have copies of architectural drawings. Those used for planning and Building Regulation approvals are quite suitable.

They will also require a detailed specification for the structural softwood, hardwood lintels (if needed), the non-structural softwood, preservative treatment, sheathing and decking, all as set out in Chapter 2.3. The details of fixings for panels will also be needed (see Chapter 1.2).

It is usually best to order all additional pieces, such as joists, noggings, decking, cavity barriers, fascias, etc from the panel supplier. These should be scheduled.

The panel supplier will usually also be prepared to supply the trussed rafters. For details needed, see Chapter 2.3.

In addition to drawings and specification, the following information needs to be given to the company.

(a) *Sizes and tolerances*

Work size for panels, joist lengths, etc, is to be 3 mm less than basic size. The tolerance on the work size is plus or minus 2 mm.

Thus, for instance, if a panel has a basic length of 2400 mm, the dimension for manufacture is 2400–3 ie 2397 ± 2 mm. That is, the panel should be not less than 2395 mm long, or more than 2399 mm long.

Such tolerances will, at the same time, limit how far panels can be 'out of square-'.

(b) *Coding of panels*

The coding of panels on drawings is to be marked on the components during manufacture.

(c) *Bracing of unsheathed panels*

It must be indicated that all unsheathed panels must have a temporary 75 mm x 25 mm diagonal brace, to prevent distortion during handling and delivery.

(d) *Details of delivery, if more than one dwelling is to be built*

If there is a number of identical houses in the order, it is most convenient for the manufacturer to make each panel type in batches. But the components will often need to be delivered in complete sets for each dwelling, with deliveries spaced out at regular intervals to suit the erection programme. If such deliveries are required, full information must be given to the company.

Do not forget to advise the manufacturer of any handed houses. (This normally only affects window/door panels).

(e) *Protection of the components from the weather*

The supplier must be informed that he is to protect the components and pieces from the weather after manufacture and during delivery. Such protection is needed to keep down the moisture content.

A well-run timber frame construction site is operated on different lines from sites where ordinary housebuilding methods are used. Also completion is speeded up, with resultant savings on overheads.

Builders with no previous experience of timber frame construction sometimes fail to recognise these facts. So do some site supervisors in local authority work. As a result, some of the advantages of timber frame construction can be thrown away. Time is lost. Quality suffers.

In this chapter we set out the main principles involved. As in other chapters we deal only with matters special to timber frame construction.

Before work starts

For each house-type, full drawings will be required. The set needed, and what each must show, is given in Chapter 2.2. There will be delays unless the information is complete.

If factory-made panels are to be used, early enquiries must be made about delivery times. These will vary widely, depending on the season and how busy is the housebuilding industry.

If panels are to be made on site, it will be necessary to take off the quantities of softwood and sheathing needed from the drawings. Timber suppliers will normally need advance notice so as to be able to organise stress grading, processing and replaning, as well as preservative treatment.

Advance ordering will also be needed for the trussed rafters. These should be on site before erection of the timber frames begins so that the building can be roofed in and made weathertight as soon as possible.

Some items special to timber frame construction, such as flexible wall ties and breather paper, are not normally stocked by builders' merchants. But they can usually supply them without difficulty provided they have sufficient warning.

Careful planning in advance is needed in all matters to ensure that there are no delays on site once work has started. Otherwise a main advantage of timber frame construction, that of speed, may be lost.

Accuracy in foundations

In ordinary housebuilding there is usually no great problem if the foundations are slightly inaccurate. The brickwork can be adjusted to suit.

In timber frame construction the aim must be to arrive

at accurately spaced studs on to which plasterboard in 1200 mm widths can be fixed without difficulty. This leaves little room for adjustment. This is especially so where factory-made panels are used. A conscious effort is needed to reach the standard required.

It is not usually possible for the initial trenchwork and concreting in the foundations to be highly accurate. But supervision is necessary to avoid gross errors.

The remaining stages of the foundation work need to be carried out with an increasing degree of accuracy.

If there is cavity brickwork or blockwork, this must be very accurately set out on the concrete and checked carefully before bricklaying starts. The coursing must be kept as level as possible.

If there is a concrete ground floor slab, the formwork needs to be checked before pouring starts. It must be level, square and true to the dimensions needed.

Final adjustment can be made when base plates or wall plates are laid. Slight dimensional errors can be made good. Mortar bedding can be slightly varied to ensure that the plates are level. Careful checking is essential before they are fixed down.

Timber and timber components on site

As we have said in the introduction, the golden rule is, use timber correctly, then the timber will take care of itself.

At no time is this so important as when timber and timber components are delivered to site. All must be carefully stacked clear of the ground, and protected from the weather.

Sequence of operations

This same need to protect the timber as much as possible applies equally during erection procedures.

As a result, the sequence of operations differs from that of other housebuilding methods. The aim should be to erect the timber frame as quickly as possible (this includes the roof structure) and then immediately protect the structure by fixing the sarking felt.

It is usually possible with an average-sized dwelling to do this within two days, using factory-made panels and a team of three carpenters.

If there is more than one dwelling, try to phase erection so that dwellings are made weathertight as soon as possible.

The structure should always be plumbed up as the work proceeds, using temporary bracing. Such bracing is also essential in case of high winds.

If decking is laid before the dwelling is weathertight — the decking should be chosen with regard to severity and length of exposure, otherwise problems may develop.

Do not remove the temporary bracing until the permanent braces in the roof are all fixed, and any upper floor decking laid.

The next stage is always to make the dwelling weathertight as soon as possible, to protect the structure permanently. This includes completing the roof finish (before this, any vent pipes and flues projecting through the roof must be positioned) and fitting windows or temporary covers over openings.

In normal housebuilding, the same scaffolding is used for both bricklaying and roofing. This may not be practicable in timber frame housing with certain conditions of cladding, if the objective of completing the roof early on is to be achieved.

Inspection stages

An important feature of the sequence of operations is a series of inspection stages. These ensure that problems do not arise later. The stages are as set out below. Note that they cover only matters which are special to timber frame construction.

Setting out of foundation trenches. Check for accuracy before foundations start.

Work above concrete strip or trench-fill bases. Check the setting out of brickwork before laying starts. Similarly, check formwork before solid ground floor slabs are laid.

Base plates or wall plates. Check level and accuracy of position before fixing.

Wall panels. Check that they are plumb and level before any upper floor joists are laid, and that they are rigidly fixed with temporary bracing. Check also before trussed rafters are fixed and braced.

Verge ladders and rafters at separating walls. Check alignment with trussed rafters before sarking felt is laid.

Completed timber structure. Check alignment generally and check against drawings, especially for extra items such as roof bracing and joist strutting, extra joists for partitions, etc. Check against fixing schedule.

Before lining out inside. Check that all service runs in wall framing and above ceilings are complete. Check that rules for notching and drilling have been followed, and that there are no runs in any separating walls. Check cavity barriers in separating walls. Check all extra pieces needed to carry plasterboard and lightweight partitions. Check extra bearers for fittings. Check the quilt in outside walls and separating walls. Check the water vapour barrier. Any holes or tears are to be made good. Taping of the barrier to penetrating services must have been carried out.

Before cladding starts. Check cavity barriers and their dpc's. Check dpc's all round openings. Check the breather paper, ensuring that this is correctly lapped in horizontal layers and with dpc's to keep the whole timber structure dry. Any damage is to be made good.

Appendix 1
Checking requirements under Building Regulations (England and Wales) 1976

Building Regulations

Reg. No.	*Requirement (simplified)*

Application to the NBA/TRADA method of timber framed housing

MATERIALS

B1   **Fitness of materials**
Materials used must be of a suitable nature and quality adequately prepared and fixed so as adequately to perform the functions for which they are designed.

The type and quality of materials, their preparation and methods of fixing, as recommended in this manual, will all meet the provisions for fitness stated in regulation B1.

B3   **Special treatment of softwood timber in certain areas**
This regulation applies only in the following areas:–
The District of Bracknell
The Borough of Elmbridge
The District of Runnymede
The Borough of Spelthorne
The Borough of Surrey Heath
The Borough of Woking
The Borough of Guildford other than the area of the former borough of Guildford
The District of Hart other than the area of the former urban district of Fleet
In the Borough of Rushmoor, the area of the former urban district of Farnborough
The District of Waverley other than the Parishes of Godalming and Haslemere
In the Royal Borough of Windsor and Maidenhead the Parishes of Old Windsor, Sunningdale and Sunninghill.

Softwood timber in roofs in these areas is to be treated with suitable preservative to prevent infestation by the house longhorn beetle.

Treatment will be deemed-to-satisfy regulation B3(2) if it meets the provisions of regulation B4, which are:–

(a) the timber is treated in accordance with BS 4072: 1974; or

(b) the timber, when freshly felled and milled and having an average moisture content of not less than 50% of its oven-dry mass, is treated by diffusion with sodium borate to produce a net dry salt retention of not less than $5.3\,kg\,m^3$ of boric acid equivalent; or

(c) the timber is completely immersed for not less than 10 minutes in an organic-solvent type wood preservative solution containing at least 0.5% gamma-HCH (hexachloro-cyclo-hexane), dieldrin or other persistent organochlorine contact insecticide and any surfaces subsequently exposed by cutting the timber for fitting into the building are thoroughly treated by dipping, spraying or brushing those surfaces with the same type of preservative.

Alternative treatments for constructional timbers are specified in BS 5268: Part 5: 1977.

PREPARATION OF SITE & RESISTANCE TO MOISTURE

C3(1) and (2)   **Protection of floors next to the ground**
Floors next to the ground to be so constructed as to prevent moisture or water vapour from ground causing damage to any part of the floor.

Regulations C4 and C5 contain provisions which are deemed-to-satisfy regulation C3(1) and (2). The provisions are based on traditional construction.

The method as given in this manual of preventing ground moisture and vapour from adversely affecting a suspended timber floor is also considered to satisfy the functional requirements of C3 (1) and (2).

C6   **Protection of walls against moisture**
All walls and chimneys must be so constructed as to prevent passage of moisture from the ground to any part of the wall itself or to any other part of the building that would be adversely affected by such moisture.

Regulation C7 states methods of protection that will be deemed-to-satisfy regulation C6. Suitable protection may be achieved by means of dpc's with continuing damp proof membranes and by using materials that are unlikely to be affected by moisture.

Such dpc's are specified in the method set out in this manual, and sill plates are required to be preservatively treated.

A dpc in an external wall is required to be not less than 150 mm above adjoining ground level.

C8   **Weather resistance of external walls**
External walls and chimneys are to be constructed to prevent rain and snow from being transmitted to any part of the building that could be adversely affected, and to prevent moisture penetration to the inside of the building.

This may readily be achieved with normal cladding techniques as set out in this manual, using a suitable breather type moisture barrier and giving careful attention to junction details.

C9   **Prevention of damp in certain cavity walls**
This regulation specifies how and where dpc's are to be provided for bridging a cavity and at jambs to openings in walls.

In a cavity wall:–

(i) Cavity to extend at least 150 mm below dpc level,

(ii) Dpc to be inserted to prevent passage of moisture from outer to inner leaf,

(iii) Vertical dpc's to be provided at openings to prevent passage of moisture from outer to inner leaf.

C10   **Weather resistance of roofs**
Roofs must be weatherproof and so constructed as not to transmit moisture to any part of the structure that could be adversely affected by it.

Suitable tile roof coverings are described in the following British Standard Code of Practice:–

On slating and tiling: BS 5534: Part 1: 1978.

STRUCTURAL STABILITY

D2

Calculation of loading
Dead and imposed loads shall be calculated in accordance with BS CP3: Chapter V: Part 1: 1967, except that, where actual static or dynamic loads will exceed the provisions for imposed loads, the design must take account of the actual loads.

Wind loads shall be calculated in accordance with BS CP3: Chapter V: Part 2: 1972.

Dead loads are based on the weights given in BS 648: 1964 "Schedule of weights of building materials".

The imposed load on any floor or roof to which there is access is taken as a uniformly distributed load of not less than 1.44 kN/m².

The actual weights of partitions must be included in the dead load unless positioning is variable or undetermined. In this case an additional load, uniformly distributed over the floor, must be included equivalent to 1 kN/m² or to one-third the weight of the partition per metre run, whichever is the greater.

The structural design rules, tables and charts in this manual take full account of the loading requirements.

D3

Foundations
(a) The foundations must be designed to transmit dead and imposed loads to the ground without causing settlement or other movement that would impair stability or cause damage to any part of the building.

(b) The foundations must be taken to sufficient depth to avoid damage by swelling, shrinkage or freezing of the subsoil.

(c) The foundations must resist chemical attack.

The low dead weight of timber framed dwellings enables foundation costs to be reduced to a minimum. This is particularly beneficial on sites where the ground has a low bearing capacity.

Timber framed dwellings are less likely to suffer damage from ground movement than are traditional buildings in brickwork or masonry. Timber framed buildings may therefore be advantageously specified for use in areas that might be subjected to mining subsidence.

Foundations will be deemed-to-satisfy if they can be shown to comply with any one of the following standards, whichever is applicable:—

(a) BS CP 2004: 1972 "Foundations"

(b) BS CP 110: 1972 "The structural use of concrete"

or

(c) BS CP 114: 1969 "The structural use of reinforced concrete in buildings".

Where strip foundations are used, they will be deemed-to-satisfy the requirements of regulation D3(a) if they comply with regulation D7 and its table.

D8

Structure above foundations
Structural parts of a building above the foundations shall safely sustain their share of the loads and transmit them to the foundations without deformation that would impair stability or cause damage to any part of the building.

Regulation D12 indicates that any structural work of timber is deemed-to-satisfy regulation D8 if it complies with:—

CP 112: Part 2: 1971.

The structural design rules, tables and charts in this manual are based on CP 112: Part 2: 1971.

STRUCTURAL FIRE PRECAUTIONS

E1

Interpretation of Section 1
E1 defines the terms used in Part E of the Regulations. Table 1 to Regulation E1 indicates methods of testing and minimum periods of fire resistance for an element of structure, door or other part of a building.

Fire resistance is defined by reference to BS 476: Part 8: 1972 "Test methods and criteria for the fire resistance of elements of building construction. Fire resistance tests meeting BS 476: Part 1: 1953 and carried out before 31st August 1973 are deemed-to-satisfy" this part.

The constructions given in this manual provide the following required fire resistances, which have either been proved by test or are based directly on deemed-to-satisfy specifications in Schedule 8 of Building Regulations 1976:—

Separating walls
60 minutes and at least 30 minutes to each leaf for load carrying purposes.

Internal loadbearing walls
30 minutes from either side.

E5

Fire resistance of elements of structure
The periods of fire resistance required for elements of structure are stated in the Tables (Parts 1 & 2) to Regulation E5.

In dwellings of not more than 2-storeys, with a floor area of not more than 500m², elements of structure in basement storeys and those which separate one dwelling from another are required to have a fire resistance of not less than 1 hour. Otherwise structural elements are required to have a fire resistance of only ½ hour.

In the case of intermediate floors the requirement is for a modified ½ hour resistance (with reduced performance as to the fire and temperature penetration of the flooring).

External walls that are 1 m or more from the boundary are required to be fire resistant from the inside only and the period of insulation, as tested to BS 476: Part 8: 1972, is limited to 15 minutes.

External walls that are within 1 m of a boundary are required to be also fire resistant from the outside.

Upper floors
30 minutes (modified).

External walls generally
30 minutes against internal fire (in all respects).

External walls clad with brickwork tile hanging or timber boarding (with plywood sheathing and 100 mm of mineral wool insulation)
30 minutes against external (as well as internal) fire.

When an external wall contains structural members which could be exposed to fire penetrating a window opening, they should be designed to resist the effects of fire. The details of construction in this manual provide for this.

E7   **External walls requirement additional to fire resistance**

External walls within 1 m of a boundary (other than those set at 80° or more to the boundary line) are required to:–

(i) Have an external surface complying with the Class 0 requirements (specified in regulation E15 (1) (e).

(ii) Have no unprotected areas greater than those permitted by Regulation E7 (1) and Schedule 10 Part 1.

External walls generally may include unprotected areas which may increase in size with boundary distances in accordance with Schedule 10 Part 1 together with Parts II or III or IV.

An "unprotected area" is defined as:–

(a) a window, door or other opening.

(b) any part of an external wall which has less fire resistance than specified by the regulations (ie 30 minutes in the case of one or two storey houses).

(c) any part of an external wall which is faced with combustible material more than 1 mm thick.

If an external wall, faced with combustible material, gives 30 minutes resistance to internal fire (as is the case with the constructions in this manual) only half the area of combustible material needs to be taken in calculating the percentage of unprotected area.

Claddings of brick and tile hanging satisfy the Class 0 requirements but timber boarding generally does not.

Unprotected areas permitted in external walls within 1 m of a boundary are very limited.

A simplified table at the end of this Appendix indicates boundary distances needed for full use of 20%, 30% and 40%, openings as allowed in Chapter 2.1 of this manual in relation to wind stability.

E8   **Separating walls**

E8(1)   A separating wall must form a complete vertical separation between buildings.

Regulations do allow very small perforatins for pipes. However, this is not considered, in this manual, to be either necessary or desirable with houses and is not recommended.

E8(3)
E8(4)   Unless a separating wall is carried above the upper surface of the roof

(i) the junction between the separating wall and the roof must be fire stopped, and

The constructional details in this manual meet this requirement.

(ii) the roof 1.5 m either side of the separating wall must be non-combustible (or have an AA, AB or AC fire rating).

The constructional details in this manual meet this requirement.

See Regulation E17 Roofs.

E8(5)   Any external wall carried across the end of a separating wall must either be bonded to the separating wall of the junction shall be fire stopped.

The constructional details in this manual meet this requirement.

See Regulation E14 for description of suitable fire stops.

E8(6)   Combustible materials must not be carried into or across a separating wall in such a way as to render ineffective its resistance to the spread and effects of fire.

The constructional details in this manual meet this requirement.

E14 Provision and construction of cavity barriers and fire stops

Cavity barriers, to prevent the passage of smoke and flames from any cavity to a room or to another cavity, are required to be provided as follows:–

(a) every cavity contained within an element shall be closed by a cavity barrier around the whole perimeter of the element and around the perimeter of any opening through the element, and

(b) if any element containing a cavity meets another such element, the cavities shall be so closed that *they do not communicate one with another.*

Any cavity within any one element except a roof which would exceed 8 m must be divided into two or more cavities such as do not exceed this dimension.

Cavity barriers in 1 and 2 storey houses should have a fire resistance of not less than $\frac{1}{2}$ hour and may be constructed of timber not less than 38 mm thick.

An element means a complete wall or floor or similar part of a building. Where there is a substantial change of direction, as at the corner of an external wall, a cavity barrier should be introduced, the two parts being regarded as separate elements.

Similarly a cavity barrier must be introduced where a cavity in a separating wall would meet one in an external wall.

Where a 2-storey house has brick cladding for the full height passing the junction between an upper floor and the timber framed wall panels, the cavities in the floor do not communicate with the cavities in the external wall because the timber plates and header joists act as cavity barriers. Care must be taken to ensure that where timber members act as fire barriers there are no gaps which would affect the integrity of the barrier.

Fire stops are to be provided to seal imperfections in fit between building elements and components and wherever services pass through elements or cavity barriers which are required to have fire resistance. The materials used for fire-stopping should be non-combustible.

The most suitable material for fire stopping, with the method of construction in this manual, is mineral wool. In some situations it is necessary to support this and/or hold it in position with galvanised chicken wire.

Further guidance on the design and installation of cavity barriers and fire stops may be obtained from

(i) BRE CP 7/77

(ii) BRE Digests Nos. 214 and 215.

E15   **Restriction of spread of flame over surfaces of walls and ceilings**

In houses of not more than two storeys, the surfaces of walls of rooms having a floor area of 4 m² or less and the surfaces of ceilings are required to be of a class not lower than Class 3. All other walls are required to have a surface not lower than Class 1.

However, areas of wall equivalent to $\frac{1}{2}$ the floor area of any room may be of Class 3 material up to a maximum of 20 m².

Surface spread of flame classifications are determined by tests to BS 476: Part 7: 1971.

Untreated rimber falls into Class 3 if it has a density of 400 kg/m³ or more. Timber, plywood and chipboard can readily be treated to achieve Class 1 surface spread of flame.

E17   **Roofs**

The performance and notional gradings of roofs are defined by BS 476: Part 3: 1975 "External fire exposure roof test".

Any roof or part of a roof is deemed to be of a specified designation if it conforms with one of the specifications set out in Schedule 9 of the Building Regulations 1976.

Roof construction of designation AA, AB or AC must be used if a building is more than 1500 m³ in capacity and consists of a terrace of 3 or more houses, except that, if the roof is 6 m to 12 m from a boundary, designation BA, BB or BC may be used. If the roof is 12 m or more from the boundary designation AD, BD, CA, CB, CC or CD may be used.

See Regulation E8(4) relating to the junction between the separating wall and a roof.

The use of concrete or clay tiled roofs as assumed in this manual satisfies the requirements in all conditions.

E18   **Small garages**

E18(6)   Small garage (floor area not exceeding 40 m²) attached to the house or forming part of it.

(a) *House complying*
    (i) Any floor over the garage must have fire resistance of not less than $\frac{1}{2}$ hour when tested from below.
    (ii) The wall separating the house from the garage must have not less than $\frac{1}{2}$ hour fire resistance when tested from the garage side.
    (iii) Any door in the wall separating the house from the garage must provide a fire resistance of not less than 30 minutes for stability nor less than 20 minutes for integrity.

         Such doors must comply with Regulation E11 and must be hung with self closing devices which may be steel rising butt hinges.

(b) *Garage complying*
    (i) The floor of the garage must be not less than 100 mm below the threshold of any door separating garage from house.
    (ii) Any external wall to the garage must provide not less than $\frac{1}{2}$ hour fire resistance.

E19   **Small open carports**

If a small garage with floor area not exceeding 40 m² is 2 m or more from any boundary and any house within the boundary, or an open carport with floor area not exceeding 40 m² and is a detached building, neither the garage nor the carport need comply with any part in Section 1 "Structural Fire Precautions" except Regulation E17 relating to the fire rating of the roof.

If a small garage (floor area not exceeding 40 m²) is less than 2 m from any house within the same boundary *either* the garage *or* the house must comply with the following requirements:–

(a) *Garage complying*
    (i) Any part of the walls of the garage within 2 m of the house shall be externally non-combustible, and
    (ii) The internal surface of the garage walls shall be of Class 0 standard.

or

(b) *House complying*

Every part of any external wall of the house which is within 2 m of the garage shall –

    (i) be externally non-combustible,

    (ii) have not less than $\frac{1}{2}$ hour fire resistance to external fire, and

    (iii) shall contain no unprotected area greater than 0.1 m² or less than 1.5 m from any other unprotected area within the wall.

If a small open carport (floor area not exceeding 40 m²) is attached to a house, the external walls of the house must comply with Regulation E7 (external walls) as though the house were alone.

THERMAL INSULATION

F3   **Maximum U-value of walls, floors, roofs and perimeter walling**

The U-value of any part of a wall, floor or roof which encloses a dwelling shall not exceed the values given in the Table to Regulation F3.

The calculated average U-value of perimeter walling (including any opening) shall not exceed 1.8 W/m²°C,

Assumed U-values for:–
Single glazing: 5.7 W/m² °C
Double glazing: 2.8 W/m² °C
Separating walls: 0.5 W/m² °C

Element	Max U-value (W/m² °C)
External wall or wall between dwelling and partially ventilated space	1.0
Floor exposed to open air or ventilated space	1.0
Roof	0.6
Perimeter walling Average U-value	1.8

Floors exposed to open air or ventilated space are not provided for within the structural rules in this manual. The space beneath a suspended ground floor which is enclosed by perimeter walls does not count as a ventilated space for the purpose of this regulation.

The recommendations in this manual regarding the incorporation of 100 mm mineral wool in all walls and ceilings beneath roofs will result in U-values in the region of:–

External wall   0.3–0.35 W/m² °C
Roof   0.3–0.35 W/m² °C

In timber framed construction U-values as good as and better than required by Building Regulations may readily be obtained by incorporating insulating materials in the cavities. Deemed-to-satisfy provisions are contained in Schedule 11 of the Regulations.

For calculation of U-values see BRE Digest No. 108 and BS CP 3: Chapter II: 1970.

A related document, BS 5250: 1975, gives "Basic data for the design of buildings: the control of condensation in dwellings".

SOUND INSULATION

G1   Any wall which separates a dwelling from another dwelling or from another building shall provide adequate resistance to the transmission of airborne sound.

The requirements of regulation G1(1) shall be deemed to be satisfied if the aggregate shortfall in sound reduction does not exceed 23 dB when the wall and its associated structure are tested to regulation G6 at the frequencies set out in regulation G2.

This regulation implies that separating walls in housing are required to provide insulation against airborne sound equivalent to Party Wall Grade. (The Party Wall Grade is based on a well built 225 mm thick solid brick wall plastered on both sides and weighing not less than 415 kg/m².)

Provided that suitable steps are taken to restrict flanking sound transmission, cavity separating walls of dry lightweight construction can achieve Party Wall Grade when constructed as follows:–

Two timber frames, each dry lined with 3 layers of 12.7 mm plasterboard with staggered joints and with a cavity not less than 225 mm between the backs of the plasterboard. A quilt of mineral wool or glass fibre not less than 25 mm thick should be fixed to one of the stud frames.

The specifications in this manual and the rule of placing windows no less than 300 mm from the end of any wall panel will ensure that adequate resistance to sound transmission is provided.

Note: This check-list is not necessarily comprehensive regarding matters other than the timber frame construction.

Simplified table of boundary distances and unprotected areas

			Approximate guide to boundary distances required by fire regulations	Minimum distances between walls and boundaries* facing them in metres			
	Particulars of Wall			Percentage of openings in walls			
Number of Storeys	Length of Wall	Type of Cladding	0%	20%	30%	40%
1	Up to and including 6 m	Brick and/or tile	0†	1.0	1.0	1.0
		Timber	1.5	2.0	2.0	2.0
	From 6 m up to 9 m	Brick and /or tile	0†	1.0	1.0	1.0
		Timber	2.0	2.5	2.5	2.5
2	Up to and including 6 m	All brick and/or tile	0†	1.0	1.5	2.0
		All timber	2.5	3.0	3.0	3.0
		Half timber half non-combustible	2.0	2.0	2.5	3.0
	From 6 m up to 9 m	All brick and/or tile	0†	1.0	2.0	2.5
		All timber	3.5	3.5	4.0	4.5
		Half timber half non-combustible	2.0	2.5	2.5	3.5

*NBA 'boundary' may be taken as the centre line of any adjacent public road, footpath, river or canal.

†Wall at boundary permitted.

This table is based on Schedule 10 of Building Regulations (1976) Parts I and II. It allows for timber cladding counting as 50% "unprotected". If openings in excess of 40% of a wall area are desired (and if it has been established that this is possible in regard to wind stability) the minimum boundary distance can be worked out from the text of Schedule 10 in the Building Regulations. In some situations use of the above table will give slightly greater distances than can be justified by direct reference to the regulations. This table is based on a 30° pitch and maximum wall length of 9 metres. Where these limits are exceeded a slight increase in boundary distance may be necessary.

Appendix 2
Checking requirements under Building Standards (Scotland) Regulations 1971

Building Regulations

Reg. No.	Requirement (simplified)

Application to the NBA/TRADA method of timber framed housing

GENERAL

A6 **Classification of buildings by occupancy**

The main body of this manual refers to buildings of occupancy sub group A1 only.

MATERIALS AND DURABILITY

B1 **Selection and use of materials**
Materials must be of a suitable quality, suitable for the purposes for which they are used, sufficiently resistant to deterioration and wear, properly prepared, and fixed in a proper manner.

The materials recommended in this manual will meet all the requirements.

STRUCTURAL STRENGTH AND Stability

C2 **Foundation and structure above the foundation**
Structure to be designed as to sustain and transmit to the foundations the combined dead and imposed loads, without deflection or deformation.

Wind loads to be calculated in accordance with BS CP3: Chapter V: Part 2: 1972. Dead and imposed loads to be calculated on the basis of the recommendations of BS CP3: Chapter V: Part 1: 1967

The loadbearing timber structure is designed in accordance with CP 112: Part 2: 1971.

Many terrace houses built in Scotland may require more than 40% openings in external walls (front and back) to give adequate daylighting (see notes to Reg. L4). This may restrict the choice of house shell.

This manual does not attempt to cover the more severe wind exposure conditions found in some parts of Scotland.

The imposed load on any floor or roof to which there is access is taken as a uniformly distributed load of not less than 1.44 kN/m². Partition loads are included in total structural loads.

STRUCTURAL FIRE PRECAUTIONS

D4 **Provision of separating walls**
Buildings must be separated by a separating wall complying with D5, D6 and D8 (below).

D5 **Requirements as to fire resistance**
Fire resistance requirements include a resistance to collapse and resistance to passage of flame and insulation. Requirements for each of these fire resistance components vary with the type and location of the element. In addition, the assumption of fire occurring from one side or either side in case of a wall, from all radial directions simultaneously for frame members or from the underside in the case of floors must be considered.

Table 5 in Schedule 9 specifies the requirements for all elements of structure (defined in Reg. A3).

The constructions described in this manual provide the following required fire resistances which have either been proven by test or are in accordance with the notional periods of fire resistance in Table 3 of the Regulations: Upper floors provide 30 minutes (modified fire resistance when the underside is exposed; external walls provide 30 minutes fire resistance when the internal side is exposed; timber framed separating walls and brick cored separating walls provide 60 minutes fire resistance when exposed from either side.

D6 **Requirements as to non-combustibility**
Separating walls and external walls within 1 m of boundary must be incombustible, but Class Relaxation Directive No. 24 allows the construction of timber separating walls.

Separating wall complies with Class Relaxation Directive No. 24 except that stud size 97 x 44 is not large enough. Thickness must be increased to 50 to agree fully with the Directive. Core walls may comply with D6 in that they provide an incombustible separating wall within the party wall. Brick-clad timber-framed walls are not usually accepted by Building Authorities when built as external walls on the boundary.

D8 **Additional requirements for separating walls**
Separating walls to form a complete vertical separation, including roof space, to be bonded and fire stopped at junctions with external walls, to be built tight to the underside of roof covering and to have no combustible material carried through the wall apart from timber sarking and underslating felt, or tiling battens solidly bedded in mortar.

The constructional details in this manual meet these requirements but see Class Relaxation Directive No. 24.

D13 **Fire stops in elements of structure of hollow construction**
Where any surface within a cavity (apart from a cavity between floor joists in a timber floor, provided that the ends of such cavities are firestopped) is of combustible material, the cavity is to be firestopped at every junction with any other cavity, and, at not

38 mm thick timber battens are used as firestops, vertically at all external corners, in the length of a wall if it exceeds 8 m and (double) at junction of separating wall external wall. Firestops are also provided around all window and door openings. Horizontal firestops are used at eaves and verges.

more than 8 m intervals horizontally and limiting the area of the cavity to 46 m².

D17 | **Distance of side of building from boundary**
No part of the side of a house shall be nearer to the boundary than one-half of the distance at which the total thermal radiation intensity in still air due to all openings in that side of the building would be 12.6 kW/m². When the radiation intensity at each such opening is 85 kW/m². (Boarded panels are treated as having an intensity of only 42 kW/m².)

Openings in an elevation facing a boundary must comply with the limitations specified in Schedule 6 and Table 8, Part II (and when applicable, Table 9).

D18 | **Roofs**
Roofs covered with bitumen felt strip slates type 2E to be kept 6 m from boundary. Roofs covered with bitumen felt slates (asbestos or fibre based), thatch or wood shingles, to be kept 12 m from boundary.

The roof coverings dealt with in this manual are of tile and not subject to these restrictions.

D21 | **Special provisions as to certain small garages and carports**
Where a garage having a floor area not greater than 40 m² is attached to a house, the dividing wall must be a fire division wall having a fire resistance of 60 min. from either side. Any access door must be a half-hour fire check door, provided with a 100 mm upstand at the threshold. If the wall of the garage is on the boundary or within 2 m of it, then it must be incombustible and only certain roof materials are permitted. If the wall of the garage is not on the boundary it must be at least 0.5 m from it.

If there is living accommodation above the garage, the floor must have 60 min. fire resistance, the external walls of the garage must be incombustible and the ceiling of the garage must be of jointless incombustible material.

The manual does not deal with timber-framed garages, nor with their integration into houses.

MEANS OF ESCAPE FROM FIRE AND ASSISTANCE TO FIRE SERVICE

E15 | **Surfaces of walls and ceilings**
Surfaces of walls in rooms and walls and ceilings of a stairway, and any passage or landing leading to it, to be of Class 1. Surfaces of ceilings generally may be Class 3 (as also may be the walls and ceilings of any room which does not exceed 4 m² in floor area). Certain percentage of aggregate area of walls and ceilings may be of Class 3.

All internal wall and ceiling linings are 12.7 mm plasterboard, which is classified Class 0.

PREPARATION OF SITES AND RESISTANCE TO THE PASSAGE OF MOISTURE

G6 | **Treatment of solum**
Solum is to be treated in such a way as to prevent the growth of vegetable matter and reduce the evaporation of moisture from the ground.

The solum is treated in accordance with the Deemed-to-Satisfy specifications (1) or (2) as the case may be.

G7 | **Resistance to moisture from the ground**
Structure in contact with ground to resist penetration of moisture.

Solid ground floor to be as specified in Deemed-to-Satisfy specification (1) and the underbuilding to a suspended timber floor to be as Deemed-to-Satisfy specification (2).

G8 | **Resistance to moisture from rain or snow**
Exposed parts of building to prevent any harmful effect of moisture from rain or snow on the health of occupants, and to restrict so far as is reasonably possible (and in the case of roofs, to prevent) the entry of moisture.

Deemed-to-Satisfy specification (5) deals with timber walls clad in timber boarding but calls for bituminous felt behind the boarding. Breather paper, as detailed in this manual should be used instead of bituminous felt. Other external claddings described in this manual can provide adequate protection when properly detailed. Slated or tiled roofs are to be laid in accordance with CP 142: 1968: Part 2: 1971.

RESISTANCE TO THE TRANSMISSION OF SOUND

H2 | **Separating walls**
Separating walls are to be constructed so that (in conjunction with other structural components) they reduce airborne sound by not less than the values given in Part I of Table II at all the frequencies given. (Party Wall Grade).

The specifications in this manual and the rules of placing windows no less than 300 mm from the end of any wall panel will ensure that adequate resistance to sound transmission is provided. Cavity separating walls of dry lightweight construction and timber-framed core walls, can achieve Party Wall Grade.

Test results for such walls are available.

RESISTANCE TO THE TRANSMISSION OF HEAT

Section 1 — Houses and Chalets

J2 | **Assumed U-values** for:–
Separating walls: 0.5 W/m² °C
Single glazing: 5.7 W/m² °C
Double glazing: 2.8 W/m² °C

J3 | **Roofs**
Thermal transmittance not to exceed 0.60 W/m² °C.

J4 **Walls**

Average thermal transmittance not to exceed 1.8 W/m² °C, and the thermal transmittance of unglazed walls not to exceed 1.0 W/m² °C.

J5 **Floors**

Ground floors to be laid upon the ground, or suspended on joists and covered with draught-resisting decking. Any floor exposed to the open air to have a thermal transmittance not exceeding 1.0 W/m² °C.

J6 **Control of interstitial condensation**

Structure to be designed so as to prevent damage to any part of the building as a result of the passage of moisture in the form of vapour from the interior of the house.

VENTILATORS

K15 **General requirements for windows and ventilators**

Top of the opening part of every window and ventilator to be at least 2 m from floor.

DAYLIGHTING AND SPACE ABOUT HOUSES

L4 Rooms shall be provided with windows so as to give the following daylight factors:

2% in kitchens over at least half the area or 4.5 m², whichever is less.

1% in livingrooms over at least half the area *and* half the depth of the room.

½% in other apartments over half the area *and* half the depth.

(Amendments to the Building Regulations are presently being considered which will simplify daylighting requirements and permit smaller windows).

The recommendations in this manual regarding the incorporation of 100 mm mineral wool in all wools and ceilings beneath roofs will result in maximum U-values in the region of:

External wall: 0.3–0.35 W/m² °C
Roof   0.3–0.35 W/m² °C

Roof construction exceeds requirements of Deemed-to-Satisfy specification (1) to regulation J3(1) except that it does not provide sarking.

Deemed-to-Satisfy specification (14b) to regulation J4(3) and J6 deals with timber framed walls clad externally with breather paper and timber boarding. The construction in this manual provides a vapour check that meets this specification and insulation that is twice the required thickness.

The heads of all structural openings for windows in this manual are 2.1 m above floor level.

Windows in the manual are restricted to maximum width and maximum head height of 2.1 m. Assuming 10% loss of width due to 'unbarred wood casements' (Table 16 of Regulations), the effective maximum width of window, for the purpose of Table 15 of Regulations is 1.89. See attached Table for the maximum size of rooms that can be lit by the largest window available in the manual.

Structural requirements may also place limitations on window sizes; see notes to Part C.

RESTRICTIONS ON SIZE OF APARTMENTS AND KITCHENS DUE TO DAYLIGHTING REQUIREMENTS

(Assuming one window per room and that the window is in the centre of one wall; window head at 2.1 m from floor, cill no higher than 1.1 m from floor and window 2.1 m wide; windows with wood frames and no glazing bars).

	area of room (m²)	min. width of room (m)
Livingrooms (ground floor)	14–15*	4.2
	13–14	3.9
	under 13	3.6
Kitchens (ground floor)	8–17	3.0
	7– 8	2.7
	6– 7	2.1
	5– 6	1.8
	3– 5	1.5
	under 3	1.2
Other apartments (ground floor)	16–17	3.6
	15–16	3.3
	14–15	3.0
	12–14	2.7
	11–12	2.4
	9–11	2.1
	under 9	1.8
Other apartments (first floor)	15–17	2.4
	12–15	2.1
	under 12	1.8

Windows narrower than 2.1 m may satisfy the requirements of some rooms. Refer to regulation Table 15.

*The window will not permit the use of a livingroom over 15 m².

Note: This check-list is not necessarily comprehensive regarding matters other than the timber frame construction.

Appendix 3
Alternative materials

Softwood

Some timber frame dwellings in the U.K. are built using Canadian softwood which has been machine-processed, before export to Canadian Lumber Standards. For this reason it is generally known in the timber trade as CLS.

Comprehensive advice on the use of such softwood is available from:
Council of Forest Industries of British Columbia (C.O.F.I.)
Templar House
81 High Holborn
London WC1V 6LS
Tel. 01 405 1105.

The general assembly methods used in this manual will still be quite suitable. The use of CLS will, however, affect the detailed dimensions, and the decision to use CLS should thus be taken at an early stage.

For instance, 89 x 38 mm construction grade Hem-Fir can only be used for studs of wall panels, if the site wind exposure and ground roughness are either: A3, A4, B4 and C4, as defined in Chapter 2.1 of this manual.

The method used in this manual to check the stability of dwellings in high winds will still be suitable. Advice will be needed, however, from COFI on the sizing of floor joists and lintels.

Sheathing

In a minority of cases alternative materials to plywood, oil tempered hardwood or high density medium board are used for sheathing in the UK for timber frame housing.

Some of these alternative sheet materials will give at least the same strength to the dwelling in resisting wind loads. Others may have only reduced strength and with these the standard method for calculating stability in high winds in this manual must not be used. In such cases, specialist advice will be essential.

Materials used must be at least as durable as Douglas Fir plywood, (external sheathing quality) and should not be liable to excessive moisture movement.

Further guidance on such alternative materials can be obtained from TRADA.

Advice on wood-fibre-based sheeting can be obtained from:
Fibre Building Board Development Organisation,
6 Buckingham Street,
London WC2N 6BZ.
Tel. 01 839 1122.

Appendix 4
Special provisions for 2-storey flats

Introduction
As a result of circulating the draft of this manual to various authorities for comment, there were strong suggestions that its usefulness would be much increased if the method could be made applicable to 2-storey flats. This appendix has therefore been prepared and included.

Various different types of timber compartment floor can provide the sound insulation and the fire resistance of 30 minutes in all respects, required by regulations*. The type on which this appendix is based was selected partly because its weight is not significantly greater than that of an ordinary upper floor and therefore the same studs and lintels as for 2-storey houses can be used. Also this type of compartment floor is considered to be less sensitive to workmanship and quality control than ones based on independent flooring laid on acoustic quilts, which also may wear or become compacted over long periods of time. It also has the advantage of enabling a firm working platform to be constructed at an early stage.

Compartment floors relying on independent ceiling joists have been used and tested in the field less extensively than other types in the British Isles, but results so far have been encouraging.

Building Regulation Requirements – England and Wales, and Scotland
There is every reason to think that the sound insulation of the floors, properly constructed on this basis, will be adequate and very probably within the tolerances allowed in field testing when suitable resilient floor coverings are provided. The fire resistance provided will be more than required for 2-storey flats. There should be little difficulty in using the construction under Building Regulations 1976, for England and Wales. However before deciding to build flats in Scotland on this basis it is advisable to check locally on the application of regulations. In Scotland, it is not the compartment floor construction which might conflict with regulations but the fact that the class relaxation for timber frame separating/compartment walls currently applies only to 2-storey houses.

However, applications for particular projects. have been favourably considered.

Alternatively, one can introduce brick or blockwork core walls into the cavities of timber framed walls between flats, using similar details to those given in this manual for 'step and stagger' situations. It can then be argued that the requirement for a non-combustible wall element between flats is met, without the need for a relaxation.

Basic Plan Arrangements
The method is suitable for main conditions shown in the adjacent diagrams covering –
(a) External common stairs
(b) Enclosed timber frame common stair elements
(c) Private stairs to upper flats within the overall plan of lower flats.

This appendix includes a range of plans prepared by the NBA (originally for another purpose) to illustrate suitable variations of the type (c) arrangement.

Construction of Private Stairways to upper flats within the overall plans of lower flats
1. The space beneath the stairs should not form part of a habitable room, because the sound insulation of the stair soffit may not be considered locally fully up to the Grade I for flats standard. However it may be used as part of a circulation space or be enclosed as a cupboard.

* Advice on alternative methods of constructing compartment floors can be obtained from TRADA. One alternative corresponds with the traditional deemed-to-satisfy specification in the Building Regulations 1976, having floating flooring and a pugged ceiling. Specification of joists, lintels and studs may have to be altered to carry the extra weight of such floors.

Conditions allowed by the Method

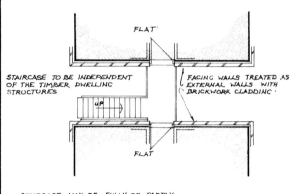

STAIRCASE TO BE INDEPENDENT OF THE TIMBER DWELLING STRUCTURES

FACING WALLS TREATED AS EXTERNAL WALLS WITH BRICKWORK CLADDING.

STAIRCASE MAY BE FULLY OR PARTLY ENCLOSED IN TRADITIONAL CONSTRUCTION INDEPENDENT OF THE TIMBER STRUCTURE

A. FLATS REACHED BY EXTERNAL STAIR

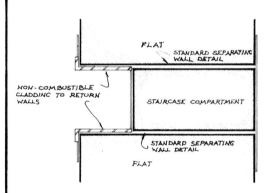

STANDARD SEPARATING WALL DETAIL

NON-COMBUSTIBLE CLADDING TO RETURN WALLS

STAIRCASE COMPARTMENT

STANDARD SEPARATING WALL DETAIL

IF STEP/STAGGER ROOF CONDITIONS RESULT FROM THE PLAN FORM, CORE WALL DETAILS FOR THE SEPARATING WALL WILL BE REQUIRED

B. FLATS REACHED THROUGH ENCLOSED TIMBER FRAMED STAIRCASE COMPARTMENT

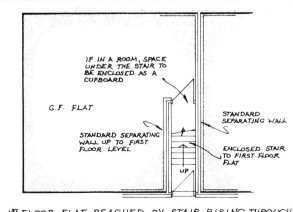

IF IN A ROOM, SPACE UNDER THE STAIR TO BE ENCLOSED AS A CUPBOARD

G.F. FLAT

STANDARD SEPARATING WALL

STANDARD SEPARATING WALL UP TO FIRST FLOOR LEVEL

ENCLOSED STAIR TO FIRST FLOOR FLAT

C. 1ST FLOOR FLAT REACHED BY STAIR RISING THROUGH GROUND FLOOR FLAT

Typical allowable flat plans where the first floor flat is reached by a stair rising through the ground floor flat

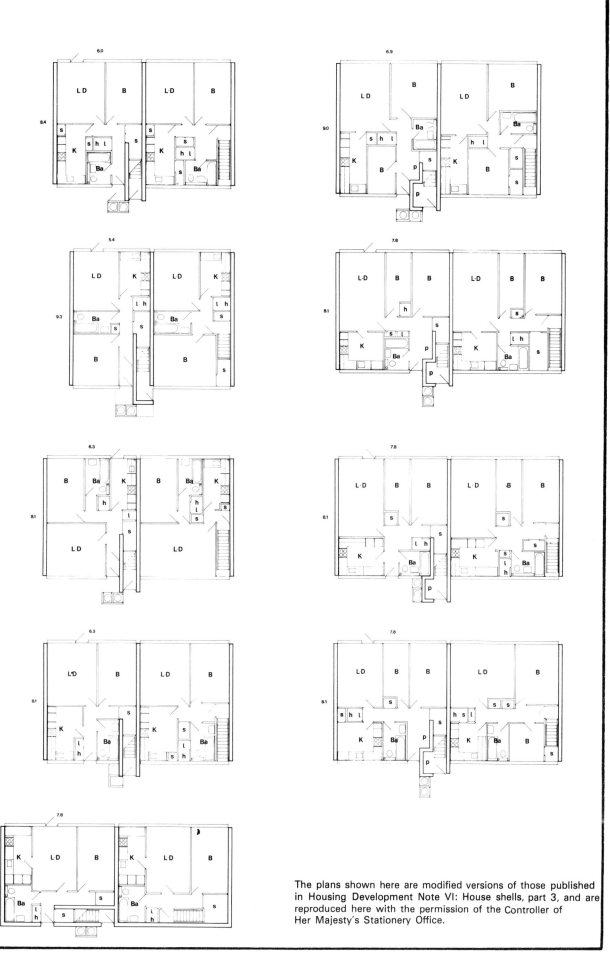

The plans shown here are modified versions of those published in Housing Development Note VI: House shells, part 3, and are reproduced here with the permission of the Controller of Her Majesty's Stationery Office.

2. The construction of the stair soffit is to be similar to that of the ceiling and extended down to floor level as shown in the illustration.

3. In some plan arrangements it may be inconvenient to introduce a 300 mm wide band of sheathing between the entrance door and a separating wall. In such cases the length of the wall with the door in it should be measured to exclude the door to obtain a notional frontage when using the wind charts in chapter 2.1 to check wind stability in relation to percentage openings. The method cannot therefore be applied to such flat frontages of less than 4.8 metres.

Construction of the Compartment Floor and Ceiling

1. Floor joist sizes are to be selected from the table of spans applicable to longer span suspended timber ground floors. This allows for the likelihood of somewhat greater (dynamic) loadings in living areas.

2. To reduce risks of flanking sound transmission the ends of floor joists have 19 x 100 notches to accommodate acoustic seating pads. The 100 x 50 x 19 pads should be pre-nailed to the joists so that the nails do not lie within the area of bearing on the timber wall plates. The pads should be type CV/M medium stress bearing pads as supplied by Textile Industrial Components Ltd. (Woking, Surrey) or equivalent approved for a working bearing pressure up to 1400 kN/m². Joist depth blockings can be fixed between joists in the normal way without serious risks of introducing structure borne sound paths.

3. To reduce risks of impact sound transmission, foam- or felt-backed plastic floor coverings should be provided in kitchen and bathroom. In other areas it is normally reasonable to presume that *occupants will provide suitable floor coverings.*

4. Load bearing intermediate internal walls in lower flats should be lined with a 19 mm layer of plasterboard on each side. This will provide for a full 30 minutes fire resistance in case the wall could be subjected to fire on both sides at the same time.

5. Ceiling joists (which should be selected from the following table), are spaced at 600 mm centres and generally located midway between and spanning in the same direction as the floor joists.

Grade of Timber	Depth of Joist (mm)	Breadth of Ceiling Joists (mm)		
		38	47	63
GS	120	3.3	3.6	3.9

SPAN OF CEILING JOISTS IN METRES (600 mm joist spacing)

The ceiling joists are notched 50 mm at the ends, but are *not* seated on acoustic pads but are securely nailed down so that they are not dislodged when the ceiling is nailed up — starting with 19 mm thick sheets against the bearing walls on each side and then working towards the middle. This will reduce any tendencies for the ceiling joists to "bounce" when nailing up to them.

Workmanship

Particular care is to be taken to ensure that no additional paths for structure borne sound are introduced by adding intermediate fixings for the suspended ceiling construction.

Details of compartment floor construction showing junctions with walls

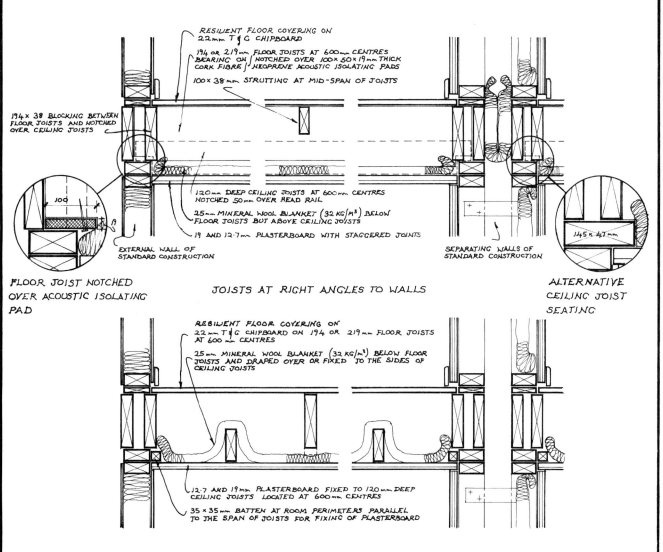

RESILIENT FLOOR COVERING ON
22mm T & G CHIPBOARD

194 or 219mm FLOOR JOISTS AT 600mm CENTRES
BEARING ON NOTCHED OVER 100 x 50 x 19mm THICK
CORK FIBRE NEOPRENE ACOUSTIC ISOLATING PADS

100 x 38mm STRUTTING AT MID-SPAN OF JOISTS

194 x 38 BLOCKING BETWEEN
FLOOR JOISTS AND NOTCHED
OVER CEILING JOISTS

100

120mm DEEP CEILING JOISTS AT 600mm CENTRES
NOTCHED 50mm OVER HEAD RAIL

25mm MINERAL WOOL BLANKET (32 KG/M³) BELOW
FLOOR JOISTS BUT ABOVE CEILING JOISTS

19 AND 12.7mm PLASTERBOARD WITH STAGGERED JOINTS

EXTERNAL WALL OF
STANDARD CONSTRUCTION

SEPARATING WALLS OF
STANDARD CONSTRUCTION

145 x 47mm

FLOOR JOIST NOTCHED
OVER ACOUSTIC ISOLATING
PAD

JOISTS AT RIGHT ANGLES TO WALLS

ALTERNATIVE
CEILING JOIST
SEATING

RESILIENT FLOOR COVERING ON
22mm T & G CHIPBOARD ON 194 or 219mm FLOOR JOISTS
AT 600mm CENTRES

25mm MINERAL WOOL BLANKET (32 KG/M³) BELOW FLOOR
JOISTS AND DRAPED OVER OR FIXED TO THE SIDES OF
CEILING JOISTS

12.7 AND 19mm PLASTERBOARD FIXED TO 120mm DEEP
CEILING JOISTS LOCATED AT 600mm CENTRES

35 x 35mm BATTEN AT ROOM PERIMETERS PARALLEL
TO THE SPAN OF JOISTS FOR FIXING OF PLASTERBOARD

JOISTS PARALLEL TO WALLS

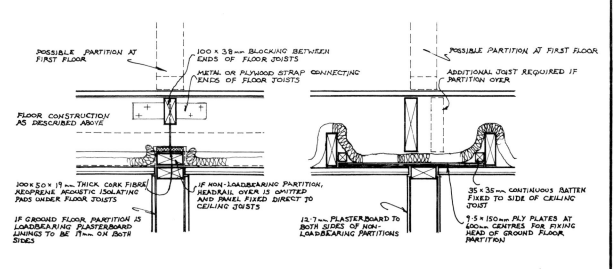

POSSIBLE PARTITION AT
FIRST FLOOR

100 x 38mm BLOCKING BETWEEN
ENDS OF FLOOR JOISTS

METAL OR PLYWOOD STRAP CONNECTING
ENDS OF FLOOR JOISTS

POSSIBLE PARTITION AT FIRST FLOOR

ADDITIONAL JOIST REQUIRED IF
PARTITION OVER

FLOOR CONSTRUCTION
AS DESCRIBED ABOVE

100 x 50 x 19mm THICK CORK FIBRE
NEOPRENE ACOUSTIC ISOLATING
PADS UNDER FLOOR JOISTS

IF NON-LOADBEARING PARTITION,
HEADRAIL OVER IS OMITTED
AND PANEL FIXED DIRECT TO
CEILING JOISTS

IF GROUND FLOOR PARTITION IS
LOADBEARING PLASTERBOARD
LININGS TO BE 19mm ON BOTH
SIDES

12.7mm PLASTERBOARD TO
BOTH SIDES OF NON-
LOADBEARING PARTITIONS

35 x 35mm CONTINUOUS BATTEN
FIXED TO SIDE OF CEILING
JOIST

9.5 x 150mm PLY PLATES AT
600mm CENTRES FOR FIXING
HEAD OF GROUND FLOOR
PARTITION

JOISTS AT RIGHT ANGLES TO INTERNAL
PARTITIONS (LOADBEARING / NON-LOADBEARING)

JOISTS PARALLEL TO INTERNAL PARTITIONS
(NON-LOADBEARING)

Details of stair rising through ground floor flat

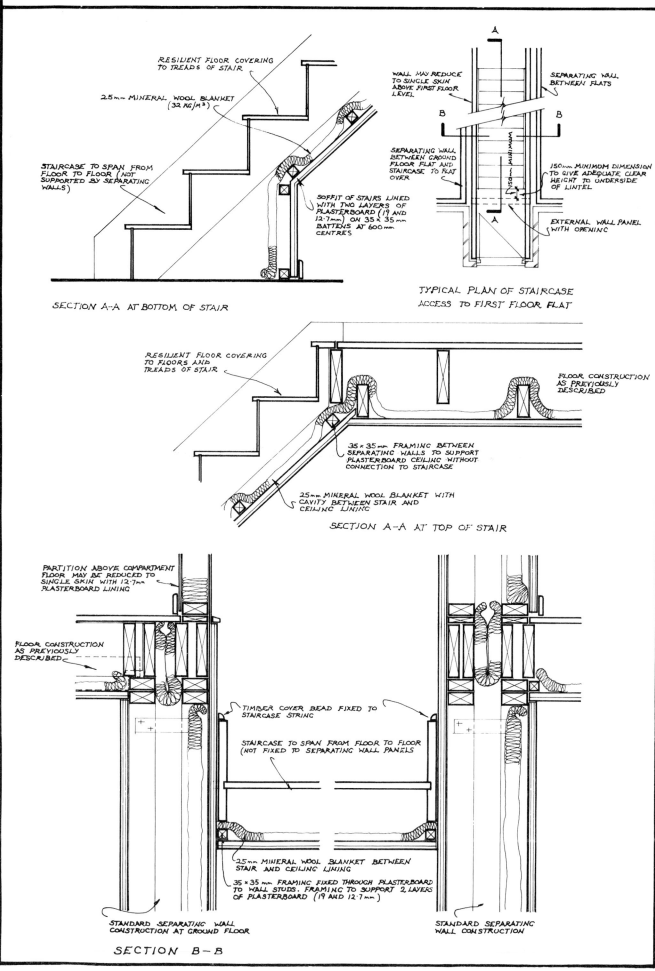

RESILIENT FLOOR COVERING TO TREADS OF STAIR

25mm MINERAL WOOL BLANKET (32 KG/M³)

STAIRCASE TO SPAN FROM FLOOR TO FLOOR (NOT SUPPORTED BY SEPARATING WALLS)

SOFFIT OF STAIRS LINED WITH TWO LAYERS OF PLASTERBOARD (19 AND 12·7mm) ON 35 × 35mm BATTENS AT 600mm CENTRES

SECTION A-A AT BOTTOM OF STAIR

WALL MAY REDUCE TO SINGLE SKIN ABOVE FIRST FLOOR LEVEL

SEPARATING WALL BETWEEN FLATS

SEPARATING WALL BETWEEN GROUND FLOOR FLAT AND STAIRCASE TO FLAT OVER

150mm MINIMUM DIMENSION TO GIVE ADEQUATE CLEAR HEIGHT TO UNDERSIDE OF LINTEL

EXTERNAL WALL PANEL WITH OPENING

TYPICAL PLAN OF STAIRCASE ACCESS TO FIRST FLOOR FLAT

RESILIENT FLOOR COVERING TO FLOORS AND TREADS OF STAIR

FLOOR CONSTRUCTION AS PREVIOUSLY DESCRIBED

35 × 35mm FRAMING BETWEEN SEPARATING WALLS TO SUPPORT PLASTERBOARD CEILING WITHOUT CONNECTION TO STAIRCASE

25mm MINERAL WOOL BLANKET WITH CAVITY BETWEEN STAIR AND CEILING LINING

SECTION A-A AT TOP OF STAIR

PARTITION ABOVE COMPARTMENT FLOOR MAY BE REDUCED TO SINGLE SKIN WITH 12·7mm PLASTERBOARD LINING

FLOOR CONSTRUCTION AS PREVIOUSLY DESCRIBED

TIMBER COVER BEAD FIXED TO STAIRCASE STRING

STAIRCASE TO SPAN FROM FLOOR TO FLOOR (NOT FIXED TO SEPARATING WALL PANELS)

25mm MINERAL WOOL BLANKET BETWEEN STAIR AND CEILING LINING

35 × 35mm FRAMING FIXED THROUGH PLASTERBOARD TO WALL STUDS. FRAMING TO SUPPORT 2 LAYERS OF PLASTERBOARD (19 AND 12·7mm)

STANDARD SEPARATING WALL CONSTRUCTION AT GROUND FLOOR

STANDARD SEPARATING WALL CONSTRUCTION

SECTION B-B

94

Appendix 5
Approval procedures

1. Introduction
In the preparation of this manual full account was taken of building regulation requirements and those of the National House-Building Council (NHBC). Drafts of the manual were sent to NHBC, to the national authorities concerned with building legislation and to organisations representing the building control professions. In all cases general comments were extremely favourable and many particular comments have been incorporated into improvements of the text. Understandably, users of this manual and the methods it contains cannot be exempted from the checking procedures that are required. However this appendix sets out what it is hoped will become a simpler and more direct path through these procedures.

2. NBA/TRADA Checking Form
NBA and TRADA have prepared a simple checking form. This can streamline the certification of timber frame structural design. Builders have to record on the form the design details based on the manual for rapid checking and certification by an Engineer.

These forms, an example of which is reproduced at the end of this appendix, are available, free of charge, from TRADA, who can provide checking and certifying services. If there are intentional (or unintentional) departures from the method, they can assist in resolving and/or justifying these, under their normal consultancy arrangements.

3. National House-Building Council Requirements
All timber frame dwellings built under the NHBC scheme must be covered by NHBC form HB 210. There are two alternatives:

A. Each timber frame dwelling type on each estate to be built by a Registered House-Builder must be assessed by a competent person such as a consulting Civil or Structural Engineer. Form HB 210 issued by NHBC must be completed by the Builder and the Engineer.

OR:

B. When standard dwelling types are to be produced for use on a number of sites, NHBC will consider giving blanket approval of the design. The designs are then appraised by an authority approved by NHBC. Where blanket approval has been given, form HB 210 must still be signed by the Builder and by an Engineer and submitted as above.

Where either of the two procedures above are followed, a competent person acceptable to NHBC must certify that the design complies with the certificate on form HB 210. It will be noted that NHBC form HB 210, certificate section D2 item (a) and (b), requires that the Engineer be satisfied that calculations and designs have been carried out in accordance with statutory requirements and the appropriate codes of practice.

The Engineer must also ensure that he is satisfied that item (c), (d) and (e), concerning constructional details, good building practice and clear production information, respectively, are met.

TRADA and NBA are both accepted by NHBC as competent authorities for the purpose of signing HB 210 certificates.

4. Building Regulations – Structural Requirements
Local authorities are empowered to call for structural calculations in support of applications, if they consider this is necessary. With designs based directly on the method set out in this manual, it is anticipated that they will, as far as superstructures are concerned, usually accept instead, the form referred to above, setting out the basic loading data and design methods derived from the "deemed-to-satisfy" timber code CP 112: Part 2: 1971, countersigned by TRADA or a suitably qualified engineer.

5. Building Regulations – Other Requirements
The methods in the manual of achieving required fire resistances and standards of sound insulation are based on a body of test results. Some local authorities may wish to examine and retain copies of such test results. Copies of appropriate test reports and certificates can be obtained, free of charge, from TRADA.

Local authorities may also ask for calculations or certificates to show compliance with thermal insulation requirements. The form prepared by TRADA includes spaces for the entry of particulars of window areas etc., to simplify the checking and certification of this matter also.

6. Further information
about the services, the forms referred to in this appendix, the underlying design methods and test information and about any changes in regulations affecting the method, is obtainable from:
Timber Research and Development Association,
Stocking Lane, Hughenden Valley,
High Wycombe, Bucks. HP14 4ND.
Tel: Naphill 3091.

NBA/TRADA TIMBER FRAME HOUSING MANUAL
A SIMPLIFIED METHOD

Design pro-forma (to be completed for each dwelling type on the site)

This pro-forma is to assist in checking that the design rules have been interpreted correctly and can form the basis of a submission for approval.

Particulars of Builder or Developer	Name _____
	Address _____
	_____
	_____
	Telephone _____
Address of Site	_____
	_____
Particulars of Certifying person or organisation	Name _____
	Address _____
	_____
	Telephone _____
	Qualification _____

CERTIFICATE I/we have checked the design referred to on this pro-forma and drawings listed below and am/are satisfied that the structural *and other** design is in accordance with the NBA/TRADA Timber Frame Housing Manual, *except in respect of matters listed in Section 1 of this form***

Signature ------------------------------ Date --------------
Name & Qualifications ------------------------------------

List of Drawings

_____   _____
_____   _____
_____   _____
_____   _____

SECTION 1 VARIATIONS Give particulars of any variations in the design from the rules and/or recommendations in the Manual (otherwise write NONE).

List and, when appropriate, attach to this form copies of documents (such as test certificates, certificates of consulting engineer or TRADA's Appraisals Section, letters of assessment or supplementary calculations) which justify variations.

(to be filled in by Builder/Developer and where appropriate added to by the Certifying Person/Organisation)	
Particulars of Variations	Justification of Variations
_____	_____
_____	_____
_____	_____
_____	_____

* delete words *and other* if structural design only is checked and certified

** delete words in italic if not applicable

SECTION 2 STRUCTURAL DESIGN DATA AND CHECKLIST

Site

Plot numbers		*including* – Detached ☐	Semi-detached ☐	Terrace ☐	✓ as applies

Minimum numbers of dwellings between steps/staggers within terraces, if any, otherwise enter NONE ☐

Site location	☐	A, B or C from wind zone map (p. 55 of Manual)

Ground roughness	☐	2, 3 or 4 from BSCP 3: Ch V: Part 2: 1972 (see page 47 of Manual)

Wind category	☐	A2, A3, A4 combination of Site location B2, B3, B4 C2, C3, C4 and Ground roughnes

Type of dwelling	☐	bungalow 2 storey house or flats

Roof pitch and span	. . . degrees . . . metres	between 22½° and 30° - roof spans up to 10.2 m between 35° and 40° - roof spans up to 8.1m

Tiling weight	kg/m²	The rules in the Manual permit - between 45 kg/m² and 55 kg/m² for roof pitches between 22½° and 30° only between 70 kg/m² and 80 kg/m² for roof pitches between 35° and 40° only

Design chart	☐	1, 2, 3, 4, 5, 6 Select chart appropriate to: 7, 8, 9, 10, 11, 12 13, 14, 15, 16 Wind category, No. of storeys and Roof pitch

Note that to comply with the rules for the use of the charts in the Manual the percentages should lie on or below the limits given in the right hand column below.

Percentage openings	front	%	rear	%	1 storey 30% 2 storeys only 30% or 40%
in external ground floor storey walls	left gable	%	right gable	%	2 storey 20% 1 storey and certain 2 storey detached 30%

Note that the percentage of openings in first floor walls must not exceed that of the wall below

Dwelling depth (length of gable)	metres	Dimensions to be within the limits of the appropriate design chart Max. roof span to be 10.2m for roof pitches of 22½ - 30° or 8.1m for roof pitches 35 - 40°
Dwelling frontage (length of eaves)	metres	Detached 2 storey dwelling with 20 - 30% openings in gable walls to occur within hatched area of design chart.

The wind chart indicates that the dwelling(s) is/are satisfactory for location on the site with internal sheathed partitions to the ground floor of each dwelling as follows:

	DET	SEMI-D	TERR			
parallel to depth				metres	3 m or ½ x depth whichever is greater	enter NONE if none required
parallel to frontage				metres	3 m or ½ x frontage whichever is greater	

Note: A detached 2 storey dwelling with 20 - 30% openings in gable walls requires 3m length of internal sheathed panel parallel to the gable (depth) in addition to that noted above. ✓ in box if this applies. ☐

SECTION 3 CHECKLIST OF MAIN PROVISIONS TO MEET FIRE, SOUND & THERMAL INSULATION, MOISTURE EXCLUSION & DURABILITY REQUIREMENTS

Give the following particulars to show that the construction is in accordance with the recommendations in the Manual, (except in respect of any matters listed in Section 3 of this form)

1. Layers of plasterboard are provided to line the frameworks as follows:

	No. of layers		✓ as applies
	19 mm	12.7 mm	
Separating walls other than any types or parts listed below:	–	3	
(a) Parts in the roof space in dwellings to be built in England or Wales	–	2	
(b) Walls at steps/staggers which include a core leaf of brick or blockwork	–	2	
(c) Ceilings of ground floor flats	1	1	
(d) Internal loadbearing partitions in ground floor flats	1	–	
(e) *All other walls and all ceilings*	–	1	

2. *Cavity barriers* are provided as follows:-

    (a) in *separating walls,* at the level of the upper floor and of the ceiling beneath the roof, at the top of the walls in the plane of the roof and at the ends of the walls where they abut the external walls

    (b) in cavities between the cladding and external wall panels around windows and doors, at the junctions of flank walls with front and back walls, at verge and roof levels

    (c) so that no cavity is longer than 8 metres

3. *Firestops* are provided:-

    (a) immediately below all roof tiles which lie above separating walls

    (b) immediately behind cladding where it passes the end of any separating wall

4. *Sound absorbent quilt* is provided:-

    (a) on at least one side of the separating wall cavity

    (b) within wall frames between bedrooms and toilets/bathrooms

    (c) over independent ceiling constructions in flats

5. *Walls close to boundaries* have limited areas of openings and/or combustible claddings so that boundary distances do not exceed those in the table at the end of Appendix 1.

6. *100 mm mineral wool insulation* is provided to an effective thickness of 97 mm. The total areas of external wall in each dwelling and the corresponding total areas of party walls and windows and the resulting average U values are as below.

	external walls	separating walls	windows	total perimeter wall area (A+B+C)	Average 'U' value of walls and windows $E = \dfrac{(A \times 0.35) + (B \times 0.5) + (C \times 5.7)}{D}$
	(A)	(B)	(C)	(D)	(E)
Mid-terrace	..... m^2	..... m^2	.... m^2	..... m^2	.... Wm^2 °C
End-terrace or semi detached	..... m^2	..... m^2	.... m^2	..... m^2	.... Wm^2 °C
Detached	..... m^2	0 m^2	.... m^2	..... m^2	...................Wm^2 °C

Note:

    (a) Divide by 2 the area of any window which is double glazed when completing Column C.

    (b) If the resulting value in column D is 1.8 or less, the current insulation requirements will be met

    (c) If the resulting value in column D is greater than 1.8 then this value can be reduced to 1.8 by reducing window area or increasing the amount of double glazing.

7. *Protection against ground moisture* is provided in accordance with the recommendations of the Manual, in the form of polyethylene sheeting not less than .024 mm thick

    (a) laid over the ground beneath the building and blinded with not less than 50 mm weak concrete (in the case of suspended timber ground floors) and/or

    (b) incorporated in or beneath the solid concrete ground floor construction

8. *Protection against moisture in external walls* is provided, in accordance with the recommendations of the Manual, by means of

    (a) breather type moisture barriers behind all claddings

    (b) flashings/dpc's around all openings

    (c) vapour barriers at the back of all inner linings to external walls

9. *Durability of timber* is safeguarded by the preservative treatment of:-

    (a) all ground storey wall plates

    (b) all joists and other timbers beneath the ground floor decking (in the case of suspended timber ground floors)

    (c) all timber cladding and windows (other than any made of the heartwood of a durable species)

    (d) all roof timbers *as required by Building Regulations as protection against House Longhorn Beetle* *

    (e) all other constructional timbers (if this is being provided although it is not an essential requirement)

*delete the passage in italics if the dwellings are not intended to be built within the areas where this is required and preservative treatment of roof timbers is still specified.

Wall stud grades	GS ☐	SS ☐	✓ as applies	GS grade except wind categories B2 and C2 where SS grade

Joists	span (m)	breadth (mm)	depth (mm)	grade	location in plan	
Ground floor	1					selected from Table 1
	2					
	3					
First floor	1					selected from Table 2
	2					
	3					

Lintel grades	65 grade Keruing 94 x 219 mm	☐ ✓ as applies	clear openings greater than 1500 mm and up to 2100 mm carrying roof load or roof load plus floor load.
	SS grade softwood 2 no. 47 x 219 mm	☐ ✓ as applies	all other lintels

CHECK LIST

Confirm, by ticking the appropriate box, that the construction complies with the following requirements, or entering N/A (not applicable)

1. Studs, floor joists and trussed rafters are at 600 mm centres and align vertically

2. Maximum clear joist span is 3.9 m.

3. Sheathed internal partitions are located in the middle third of the plan

4. Openings in external wall panels are at least 300 mm from the ends of frames and other openings in the same frame (see appendix for interpretation of this rule with regard to flats.)

5. All loadbearing wall frames are at least 1.8 m and not more than 3.6 m long

6. Cripple studs are provided to lintels (2 cripple studs each end of lintels spanning more than 1.8 m)

7. Maximum length of any opening in an external wall is 2.1 m

2 storey dwellings only

8. Except at stair wells, first floor joist ends are supported on load bearing panels

9. 'Staggered' openings as defined in the NBA/TRADA Manual do not occur

10. The stairwell is in accordance with the NBA/TRADA Manual

11. There are no structural overhangs or set backs at first floor level

1 storey dwellings only

12. Roofs span the shorter distance between external walls

13. In L-shaped dwellings, trusses are supported internally on load bearing panels

Note: Although not covered by the NBA/TRADA Manual the adequacy of the design of trussed rafters must also be checked/confirmed (for NHBC and probably also building control purposes).

Appendix 6
Glossary

This short glossary sets out the meaning of the few technical terms special to timber frame construction, *as used in this manual.*

Barrier

cavity barrier — A barrier used to prevent the spread of fire in cavities composed of 38 mm thick softwood in outside walls, and 50 mm thick mineral wool, wire reinforced, in separating walls.

moisture barrier — A membrane fixed to the outside face of sheathing, protecting it from any rainwater that may penetrate the cladding. Breather paper to BS 4016: 1966 is used. This is permeable, so condensation does not form on its inside face.

vapour barrier — An impermeable membrane put on to the inside face of outside wall frames to prevent condensation within the walling. It consists of polyethylene sheeting fixed before plasterboard linings are mounted or an aluminium foil backing to the plasterboard sheets.

Binder

head binder — A continuous softwood piece fixed on to the top plate of wall frames; it binds the wall frames together. It is used throughout to carry upper floor joists and trussed rafters, but is not used under spandrel frames in gable walls or separating walls.

97 x 44 mm pieces are used.

Blocking — Short pieces fixed between joists. Holds the ends of joists in position over wall frames. Use 38 mm thick pieces, the same depth as the ends of the joists.

Breather paper — See Barrier, moisture.

Bracing

roof — Permanent bracing fixed to trussed rafters to make the roof structure stable.

separating wall — Permanent bracing fixed to wall frames used in separating walls. Carries wind loads on front and rear walls of the dwelling.

temporary — Used during erection to plumb up the timber structure. Also protects the structure from collapse in high winds. Removed only after structure is complete, including roof bracing and any upper floor decking.

Claddings — External finish to outside walls. Always used in such a manner as to create a cavity between it and the breather paper protecting the timber structure.

heavyweight cladding — Brickwork or blockwork. Not carried on the timber structure but built directly off the foundations. Requires separate lintels over openings. Flexible wall ties are used to allow slight vertical movement between cladding and timber structure. For the same reason movement gaps are allowed under window sills, eaves and verges.

lightweight cladding — Horizontal shiplap boarding, or vertical tile hanging. Carried off the timber structure on battens.

Coding — Usually simple numbering of wall frames. Used to identify each frame on the drawings, during manufacture and on site.

Decking — Flooring fixed to joists. May be tongued and grooved softwood, plywood, or a suitable grade of chipboard.

Dwangs — See Noggings.

Fire stop — Non-combustible material used to seal a joint against the spread of fire. Needed over separating walls when laying slates or tiles. Also needed round chimneys, flues and pipes that penetrate ceilings and floor decking.

Frames

wall — Frames that form part of the timber structure. Made up of vertical studs at 600 mm centres, top plates and bottom plates, using 97 x 44 mm pieces throughout.

spandrel — Triangular frames used in gable walls and separating walls to form part of the roof structure.

Joist hangers — Metal connectors used to carry trimmed joists on trimmers, and trimmers on trimming joists. Avoids need for jointing.

Joists

common — Timbers spanning between wall frames to form floors. Always set out at 600 mm centres.

trimmed — Joists parallel to the common joists but cut to form a stairwell carried on a trimmer.

trimming — Joists at a stairwell parallel to common joists. Carry trimmer.

Lintels — Needed over any opening in wall frames where studs are cut. Must be directly carried at each end on extra studs, known as cripple studs. Two 219 x 97 mm pieces of SS grade timber are used unless Chapter 2.1 calls for a 219 x 97 mm hardwood lintel.

Needed over openings in heavyweight claddings. Use galvanised mild steel angle or approved proprietary metal lintel.

Nails

common — Nails to BS 1202: Part 1: 1974 suitable for most fixings in timber frame structures built in accordance with this manual.

masonry	Toughened nails used to fix base plates and wall plates down to the substructure.
shot-fired	Nails which are mechanically fired, used to fix base plates and wall plates down to the substructure.
Noggings	Horizontal softwood pieces fixed between studs and joists (called 'dwangs' in Scotland)
	44x44mm pieces are used to carry the edges of plasterboard linings and for fixtures and fittings.
Packing piece	A 97x22mm continuous piece (or as depth of decking) used to pack up wall frames over floor joists.
Pitch	The slope of a roof in degrees from the horizontal.
Plate	
base	A continuous 97x60mm piece, fixed to the foundation on a dpc, on which the timber frame is erected.
bottom	The bottom member of a wall frame.
top	The top member of a wall frame.
wall	A continuous 97x60mm piece fixed to the foundation walls on a dpc to carry suspended timber ground floors.
Preservative treatment	One of the methods recommended in BS 5268: Part 5: 1977 to protect softwood against fungal and insect attack.
	Must be used for base plates, cavity barriers and any battens fixed outside the breather paper. Must also be used for all softwood used for suspended ground floors. In some areas of SE England must be used for trussed rafters and all other pieces in the roof, to prevent attack by longhorn beetles.
	Treatment of all softwood in timber frame buildings is not essential otherwise, but is recommended.
Rafters	
trussed	Triangulated roof components set out at 600mm centres to form the roof. Must be adequately braced. Normally designed by the supplier, to the requirements of CP 112: Part 3: 1973.
loose	Used on spandrel panels in separating walls to complete the roof.
Schedule of fixing	List of all fixings needed to erect the timber structure. Must be followed to ensure stability.
Separating wall	Wall between two dwellings.
Sheathing	Sheeting fixed to wall frames. Used throughout on outside walls it strengthens the structure to carry wind loads. Can also be used on suitable internal wall frames to increase stability in high winds. In this manual 8mm plywood, 6.4mm oil tempered hardboard or 9mm high density medium board of suitable specifications may be used in 1.200m wide sheets.
	Alternatives are possible.
	See Appendix 3.
Softwood	
stress graded	Pieces which have been graded, either visually or by machine, to exclude those with excessive defects. This is done to the rules set out in BS 4978: 1973.
	GS grade (General Structural) and SS grade (Special Structural) timbers are used as specified in Chapter 2.3 of this manual.
sawn	Timber sawn to size, not planed or otherwise finished.
processed	Sawn timber machine planed on all four faces. Used for all wall framing for greater accuracy.
regularised	Sawn timber used for joists where the top and bottom faces are machine planed for greater accuracy. Used throughout for all joists.
Studs	Vertical members of wall frames.
	97x44mm pieces are used set out at 600mm centres.
cripple	Extra studs always used to carry the ends of lintels in wall frames.
Strutting	Pieces used to connect floor joists more than 2.500 metres long at mid-span to prevent overturning.
Size	
basic	The dimension into which a timber piece or component must fit. In this manual horizontal basic sizes are always a multiple of 100mm. Used to be called nominal size, a term now deprecated.
work	The size to which suppliers must work. Is always less than the basic size, to allow tolerances. Used to be called manufacturing size, a term now deprecated.
Trimmer	Joists at right angles to common joists at a stairwell. (Carries trimmed joists).
Verge ladder	Framing to carry the roof over gable walls.

Appendix 7
Bibliography

1. British Standards Institution. *Specification for nails: Part 1. Steel nails.* British Standard BS 1202: Part 1. London, BSI. 1974.

2. British Standards Institution. *Factory-made insulated chimneys: Part 2. Chimneys for solid fuel fired appliances.* British Standard BS 4543: Part 2. London, BSI. 1976.

3. British Standards Institution. *Factory-made insulated chimneys: Part 3. Chimneys for oil fired appliances.* British Standard BS 4543: Part 3. London, BSI. 1976.

4. British Standards Institution. *Code of basic data for the design of buildings. Chapter V. Loading. Part 2. Wind loads.* British Standard Code of Practice CP 3: Chapter V: Part 2. London, BSI. 1972.

5. British Standards Institution. *Timber grades for structural use.* British Standard BS 4978. London, BSI. 1973.

6. British Standards Institution. *Dimensions for softwood: Part 1. Sizes of sawn and planed timber.* British Standard BS 4471: Part 1. London, BSI. 1978.

7. British Standards Institution. *Code of practice for the structural use of timber: Part 5. Preservative treatments for constructional timber.* British Standard BS 5268: Part 5. London, BSI. 1977.

8. Canadian Standards Association. *Douglas fir plywood.* CSA Standard 0121–M1978. Rexdale, CSA. 1978.

8. American Plywood Association. *US Product Standard PS I–74 for construction and industrial plywood with typical APA grade-trademarks.* Tacoma, APA. 1974.

10. British Standards Institution. *Specification for building papers (breather type).* British Standard BS 4016. London, BSI. 1972.

11. British Standards Institution. *Code of practice for the structural use of timber. Part 3. Trussed rafters for roofs of dwellings.* British Standard Code of Practice CP 112: Part 3. London, BSI. 1973.

12. British Standards Institution. *Grading and sizing of softwood flooring.* British Standard BS 1297. London, BSI. 1970.

13. British Standards Institution. *Wood chipboard and methods of test for particle board.* British Standard BS 5669. London, BSI. 1979.

14. British Standards Institution. *Gypsum plasterboard.* British Standard BS 1230. London, BSI. 1970.

15. Canadian Standards Association. *Canadian softwood plywood.* CSA Standard 0151–M1978. Rexdale, CSA. 1978.

16. British Standards Institution. *The structural use of timber: Part 2. Metric units.* British Standard Code of Practice CP 112: Part 2. London, BSI. 1971.

17. British Standards Institution. *Wood preservation by means of water-borne copper/chrome/arsenic compositions.* British Standard BS 4072. London, BSI. 1974.

18. British Standards Institution. *Schedule of weights of building materials.* British Standard BS 648. London, BSI. 1964.

19. British Standards Institution. *Code of practice for slating and tiling: Part 1. Design.* British Standard BS 5534: Part 1. London, BSI. 1978.

20. British Standards Institution. *Code of basic data for the design of buildings. Chapter V. Loading. Part 1. Dead and imposed loads: metric units.* British Standard Code of Practice CP 3: Chapter V: Part 1. London, BSI. 1967.

21. British Standards Institution. *Code of practice for foundations.* British Standard Code of Practice CP 2004. London, BSI. 1972.

22. UK Parliament. *Building and buildings.* The Building Regulations 1976. Statutory Instruments 1976 No. 1676. London, HMSO. 1976. (As amended).

23. Building Research Establishment. *Standard U-values.* Digest 108. London, HMSO. 1975.

24. British Standards Institution. *Code of basic data for the design of buildings: The control of condensation in dwellings.* British Standard BS 5250. London, BSI. 1975.

25. UK Parliament. *Building and buildings.* The Building Standards (Scotland) (Consolidation) Regulations 1971. Statutory Instruments 1971 No. 2052 (S.218). London, HMSO. 1971. (As amended).

26. British Gas. *Gas in housing, a Technical guide.* British Gas Regional Housing Development Departments. 1978.

Further Reading

1. Timber Research and Development Association. *Timber and the Building Regs.* Hughenden Valley, TRADA. 1977.

2. Timber Research and Development Association. *Timber frame house construction.* TRADA Library Bibliography TLB 210. (Contains selected references to world literature held by the TRADA Library).

3. British Woodworking Federation. *Guide to wood windows.* Wood Information, Section 1. Sheet 8. London, BWF. 1977.

4. Swedish Finnish Timber Council and British Woodworking Federation. *Knowing your timber framed house.* Retford, SFTC & London, BWF. 1978.

5. Timber Research and Development Association. *Care of timber and wood based products on building sites.* Wood Information, Section 4. Sheet 12. Hughenden Valley, TRADA. 1976.